Schriften zur
Europäischen Integration und
Internationalen Wirtschaftsordnung

Veröffentlichungen des
Wilhelm Merton-Zentrums für Europäische Integration und
Internationale Wirtschaftsordnung,

edited by

Professor Dr. Dr. Rainer Hofmann, Universität Frankfurt a. M.
Professor Dr. Stefan Kadelbach, Universität Frankfurt a. M.
Professor Dr. Rainer Klump, Universität Frankfurt a. M.

Volume 47

Stefan Kadelbach (ed.)

Brexit – And What It Means

Nomos

The Deutsche Nationalbibliothek lists this publication in the
Deutsche Nationalbibliografie; detailed bibliographic data
are available on the Internet at http://dnb.d-nb.de

ISBN   978-3-8487-6012-1 (Print)
        978-3-7489-0132-7 (ePDF)

British Library Cataloguing-in-Publication Data
A catalogue record for this book is available from the British Library.

ISBN   978-3-8487-6012-1 (Print)
        978-3-7489-0132-7 (ePDF)

Library of Congress Cataloging-in-Publication Data
Kadelbach, Stefan
Brexit – And What It Means
Stefan Kadelbach (ed.)
135 p.
Includes bibliographic references.

ISBN   978-3-8487-6012-1 (Print)
        978-3-7489-0132-7 (ePDF)

1st Edition 2019
© Nomos Verlagsgesellschaft, Baden-Baden, Germany 2019. Printed and bound in
Germany.

Preface

Brexit dominates the political debate in Britain and often also in Europe, but even as the date for an unregulated Brexit approaches, the consequences are all but clear. What does Brexit mean for Britain's status vis-à-vis the single market? What happens to Union citizens living in Britain or British nationals residing in the EU? Has Brexit changed the political culture in the United Kingdom and how does it affect the shape of the European Union? And which prospects are there for future relations between UK and EU? These are the questions discussed during the 17th Walter Hallstein Symposium hosted by the Wilhelm Merton Centre for European Integration at Goethe University Frankfurt am Main on March 15 and 16, 2018. The present volume presents most of the contributions to this conference. The papers have been updated until November, partly until December 2018.

The conference was generously supported by the Fritz Thyssen Foundation to which the organizers are most grateful. We also owe thanks to *Sascha Gourdet* and *Raven Kirchner* for the thorough editing of the manuscripts.

Frankfurt am Main, January 2019

Rainer Hofmann   Stefan Kadelbach   Rainer Klump

Content

Brexit – And What It Means

Stefan Kadelbach

A.   *The Path to "Brexit"*

On June 23, 2016, a referendum was held in the United Kingdom, following an announcement made by then Prime Minister David Cameron in 2013, about continuing membership of the country in the European Union.[1] A majority of 51.9 per cent voted for "leave", against 48.1 per cent who favoured to "remain".[2] The outcome is not formally binding in legal terms, but it is treated as a mandatory commitment within the political system. After the Supreme Court of the United Kingdom had ruled that the notification by the government to the EU to leave required an Act of Parliament[3] and after Parliament had passed the Notification of Withdrawal Act,[4] Prime Minister Theresa May gave the notice provided for if a Member State decides to withdraw for the EU in March 2017.[5] The procedure triggered by that declaration is further spelled out in Article 50 TEU: The EU and the withdrawing state are to negotiate a withdrawal agreement, which also takes account of the future relationship between the parties. If no such agreement is achieved, membership ends two years after the notification of the intention to withdraw, if that period is not extended by unanimous vote of the European Council (Article 50(2) and (3) TEU). For Brexit, this two years' time span would expire March 29, 2019.

---

1   On the initial course of events, see *Craig*, Brexit: A Drama in Six Acts, EL Rev. 41 (2016), 447 ff.
2   The Electoral Commission, EU referendum results, www.electoralcommission.org.uk/find-information-by-subject/elections-and-referendums/past-elections-and-referendums/eu-referendum/electorate-and-count-information, last accessed 10 December 2018, like all online material cited in this introduction.
3   *R (Miller) v Secretary of State* [2017] UKSC 5.
4   An Act to Confer power on the Prime Minister to notify, under Article 50(2) of the Treaty on European Union, the United Kingdom's intention to withdraw from the EU, 2017 c. 9, effective 16 March 2017.
5   Available at www.gov.uk/government/publications/prime-ministers-letter-to-donald-tusk-triggering-article-50, dated 29 March 2017.

The future status of EU law and of the jurisprudence of the Court of Justice of the European Union (CJEU) in British domestic law is specified in the European Union (Withdrawal) Act.[6] Further legislation is expected, but its contents will depend on the fate of the negotiated withdrawal agreement. A draft text of such an agreement of 585 pages was agreed on November 14, 2018, its entry into force is envisaged for March 30, 2019.[7] The draft treaty follows a two-phase approach in that it provides for a period of transition from the time of stepping out of the EU until the end of 2020 (Article 126) and, but leaves political and economic relations between the parties after the end of the transition period to further agreement (Article 184). Apart from housekeeping issues and the phasing out of ongoing programmes and financial obligations, it contains certain assurances for the status of Union citizens, migrant workers and self-employed persons, as well as rules for providing services and matters of social security. Other issues are explicitly agreed on a transitional basis, such as free movement of goods and cooperation in police and justice affairs. Additional protocols deal with the border between Northern Ireland and the Republic of Ireland, the British military bases in Cyprus, the status of Gibraltar, and catalogues of secondary law and their application in various fields.

The agreement needs approval from both sides. The heads of states and governments of EU 27 present in the European Council "endorsed" the draft withdrawal treaty,[8] but the agreement is yet to be signed and ratified. Even though the question is not fully settled whether the agreement has to be ratified not only by the EU, but also by its Member States, the better arguments advocate in favour of an "EU only" agreement as it merely regulates transitory relations until the exit becomes fully effective.[9] In contrast to Article 49

---

6   An Act to Repeal the European Communities Act 1972 and make other provision in connection with the withdrawal of the United Kingdom from the EU, 2018 c. 16, effective 26 June 2018; see the contribution by *Anthony Arnull* in this volume.
7   Draft Agreement on the withdrawal of the United Kingdom of Great Britain and Northern Ireland from the European Union and the European Energy Community, as agreed at negotiators' level on 14 November 2014, TF50 (2018) 55 – Commission to EU27, ec.europa.eu/commission/sites/beta-political/files/draft_withdrawal_agreement_0.pdf.
8   European Council, Conclusions of 25 November 2018, EUCO XT 20015/18, BXT 110 CO EUR 27, CONCL 8.
9   To the same result see *Eeckhout and Frantziou*, Brexit and Article 50 TEU: A Constitutionalist Reading, CML Rev. 54 (2017), 695, 717 f.; cf. *Dougan*, An Airbag for the Crash Test Dummies? EU-UK Negotiations for a Post-withdrawal "Status Quo" Transitional Regime under Article 50 TEU, CML Rev. 55 (2018) Special Issue, 57, 86 f.

TEU, which provides for ratification "by all contracting States in accordance with their respective constitutional requirements" for accession agreements with new candidate Member States, such a clause is missing in Article 50 TEU. Otherwise, individual states could veto a withdrawal, which would run counter the intention of allowing states to leave the EU at their will.[10] This view also complies with state practice with regard to the termination of international treaties, which usually takes place without parliamentary participation. As a result, the acceptance of the EU to the withdrawal agreement does not seem to be difficult to obtain.

Regarding the United Kingdom, by contrast, when this introduction is being written in autumn 2018, assent is still far from certain. If the agreement should not find approval in Parliament before March 29, 2019, three outcomes are possible: First, an unregulated exit, as foreseen by Article 50(3) TEU, a radical version of the so-called "hard Brexit". Second, the Council decides to extend the time-limit of two years by unanimous vote. And thirdly, even though not likely, a new referendum; whereas the Supreme Court of the United Kingdom has left the question open whether it is legally feasible if the UK could revoke its withdrawal, the European Court of Justice held that it could.[11]

B.   Consequences of Withdrawal for the EU

Observers of Brexit may point to the fact that the United Kingdom has always had a special position with regard to, and within, the European Union. *Churchill's* notion of a federation of European States, famously, did not include Britain.[12] The European free trade area organised in the framework of EFTA on British initiative was meant as an alternative design to the European Economic Community and its finality of an ever-closer integration.[13] As early as 1975, only few years after the accession to EEC, a first referendum on an exit was held.[14] Substantial reservations have applied to a wide range

---

10   For the same reason, the vote in the European Council on the withdrawal agreement requires qualified majority, but not unanimity (Article 50(2) TEU).

11   ECJ, *Wightman et al.*, Case C-621/18, EU:C:2018:999.

12   A recording of the famous address at the Congress of Europe in The Hague on 7 May 1948 is found at www.cvce.eu/en/obj/address_given_by_winston_churchill_at_the_congress_of_europe_in_the_hague_7_may_1948-en-58118da1-af22-48c0-bc88-93cda974f42c.html.

13   *Judt*, Postwar – A History of Europe since 1945, 2005, p. 307.

14   Documented in *Butler and Kitzinger*, The 1975 Referendum, 1976.

of policies, such as the fishing privileges agreed upon in the wake of Britain's accession to the EEC.[15] Also in other areas, Britain claimed opt-outs at least temporarily, as it was the case with the Charter of social and workers' Rights in 1989,[16] if not permanently. Explicit exceptions still apply to the calculation of Britain's contribution to the common budget,[17] the Economic and Monetary Union,[18] fundamental rights,[19] free movement of Union citizens,[20] and the cooperation in migration, asylum, justice and home affairs including the Schengen system.[21] In the past years, the British representative in the Council of Ministers enhanced the number of negative votes and thereby reduced the amount of unanimous decisions in this institution from 80-90 to 65 per cent,[22] thus reacting on the role of an increasingly eurosceptic rhetoric in English domestic politics since the early 1990s. Britain has not shared the emotional commitment to Europe as a peace project that had carried much of European integration for decades,[23] and one dare say that it has never been a full member of the European Union. Brexit did not come as a surprise, given the importance criticism of the EU had gained as an argumentative pattern in British

---

15 The fisheries reservations have been prolonged as secondary law regularly, see Regulation (EU) on the Common Fisheries Policy, OJ 2013 L 345/22, Article 5(2), valid until 31 December 2022.

16 Community Charter of Social Rights, COM (89) 248 final of 30 May 1989.

17 Council Decision on the system of own resources of the European Union, OJ 2014 L 168/105, Article 5.

18 Protocol (No. 15) relating to the United Kingdom of Great Britain and Northern Ireland, OJ 2008 C 115/284.

19 Protocol (No. 30) on the Application of the Charter of Fundamental Rights of the European Union to Poland and to the United Kingdom, OJ 2008 C 115/313.

20 Protocol (No. 20) on the Application of Certain Aspects of Article 26 of the Treaty on the Functioning of the European Union to the United Kingdom and Ireland, OJ 2008 C 115/293.

21 Protocol (No. 21) on the Position of the United Kingdom and Ireland in respect of the Area of Freedom, Security and Justice, OJ 2008 C 115/295; Protocol (No. 19) on the Schengen Acquis into the Framework of the European Union, OJ 2008 C 115/290.

22 *van Aken*, Voting in the Council of the European Union: Contested Decision-Making in the EU Council of Ministers (1995-2020), Swedish Institute for European Studies, Report 2012:2, pp. 45, 59; *Haltern*, Europarecht – Dogmatik im Kontext, Vol. I, 3rd ed. 2017, paras. 322 ff., 1106.

23 *Edward*, "In Europe, History is the Unseen Guest at Every Table", CML Rev. 55 (2018) Special Issue, 251 ff.

day-to-day politics. Thus, some even see Brexit as an opportunity to reaffirm the identity of the EU and its constitutional principles.[24]

However, it would be premature to conclude that the withdrawal of Great Britain from the EU will entail predominantly positive effects on its constitutional structure or facilitate a reassessment of the finality or the political and constitutional orientation of European integration.[25] Taking into account the general political climate in many Europe states these days, this is not even a convincing prediction for the functionality of the Union's institutions. What is certain, however is that the EU will have to rearrange its balance: The voting weight of the Member States in Council decisions will change and give larger members yet more influence. The effect of strengthening large Member States will only in part be compensated by the redistribution of seats in the European Parliament, for which the upper ceiling of 96 mandates per country will be upheld, whereas some smaller states gain additional seats.[26] Many minor issues, such as the use of languages within the institutions will be discussed.[27]

More important than such modifications in numbers and institutional practice, however, are the potentially detrimental effects on the economy[28] and the changes in the political culture within the EU[29] that Brexit might entail. The United Kingdom is one of the important players relying on an economic – rather than political – role of the EU and of a free, private competition-based market economy, so that the representatives of different economic and

---

24   *Pernice*, Brexit – Exercise of Democracy or a Challenge to Democracy? WHI – Paper 03/2017, 16 f.; *Hillion*, Withdrawal under Article 50 TEU: An Integration-friendly Process, CML Rev. 55 (2018) Special Issue, 29 ff.

25   The exhortation to do so is a *leitmotif* in many German contributions to the Brexit Supplement in GLJ 17 (2016), see the pleas for more subsidiarity by *Di Fabio*, at 21 ff., *Heinig*, at 29 ff., *Nettesheim*, at 87 ff., and *Schorkopf*, at 95 ff.; but see conclusions drawn from a more integrationist perspective by *Möllers*, at 71 ff., and *Somek*, at 105 ff.

26   European Council decision establishing the composition of the European Parliament, OJ 2018 L 165 I/1.

27   *Pingel*, Le *Brexit* et le régime linguistique des institutions de l'Union européenne, RTDEur 2017, 657 ff.

28   For the effects on the German and European economy see *Felbermayr et al.*, Öko-nomische Effekte eines Brexit auf die deutsche und europäische Wirtschaft – Studie im Auftrag des Bundesministeriums für Wirtschaft und Energie, Munich 2017, available at www.bmwi.de/Redaktion/DE/Publikationen/Studien/oekonomische-effekte-eines-brexit-auf-die-deutsche-wirtschaft.pdf?__blob=publication-File&v=6.

29   See the contribution by *Matthias Ruffert* in this volume.

social models will balance out themselves against the remaining market-liberal orders anew. What that means will depend on the political agendas of the remaining states, but the withdrawal of Britain could prove a loss of a counterweight to other individual ambitions.

C.   Consequences of Brexit for the United Kingdom

Again, obvious effects of Brexit will most likely be seen in the economy. Even though predictions are debated both in Europe and Britain, the probable outcome appears to be that the British economy will suffer substantial loss.[30] As opposed to such forecasts, which basically rest on model simulations, effects on the political and constitutional system are much more difficult to predict. Whereas Brexiters like to think – or at least to say – that withdrawal will entail a strengthening of sovereignty, independence and control, others draw a gloomy picture. Accordingly, Brexit has already changed the political culture in Britain in that it divided the population into two irreconcilable camps, shifted representative democracy towards a majoritarian, if populist mode of decision-making, contributes further to an erosion of trust in politics, and threatens the pluralist and liberal character of Britain's law and society by removing constraints on executive power that derive from supranational and international law.[31]

From all problems Brexit poses to the United Kingdom, the future fate of devolution is one of the most salient.[32] In Scotland and Northern Ireland, the majority of the population voted for "remain".[33] For Scotland, the question of leaving Britain (and perhaps of joining the EU) has been raised again, but a new referendum seems unlikely.[34] Since Scotland has no voice in the Brexit procedure but has to bear with the results, the whole process can be interpreted as a decrease of its autonomy. For Northern Ireland, the fact of having

---

30   For the effects on trade see *Felbermayr et al.* (above note 28), at 79 ff.
31   See the contribution by *Mark Dawson* in this volume.
32   See the contribution by *Gordon Anthony* in this volume.
33   Above note 2.
34   Since re-entry into the EU after secession might be burdensome (but see *Stoffels*, EU-Mitgliedschaft und Abspaltung, Baden-Baden 2017, who advocates for a right of re-entry under EU law for regions which secede on a consensual basis) and Scotland would not necessarily keep its most important market, England, on equal conditions, Brexit has not made Scottish independence more likely, see *Schieren*, Die schottischen Unabhängigkeitsbestrebungen nach dem Brexit-Votum: neue Lage bei getrübten Aussichten, integration 2017, 193, 205 f.

been outvoted by an English majority may entail even more serious consequences. For this part of the Union, to leave the internal market in a hard Brexit variant would mean to re-introduce border control at the frontier to Ireland and to create the conflict again between Unionists and Republicans which the Good Friday Agreement of 1998 had settled.[35] The agreement sets out that Northern Ireland and the Republic of Ireland are "partners in the European Union",[36] affirms human rights and non-discrimination on the fundament of the European Convention of Human Rights, and presupposes free movement across frontiers. The Draft Withdrawal Agreement addresses this special situation in an additional protocol that provides for a transitional status and envisages a treaty of its own. It promises to safeguard individual rights, and it defines the area as a "common travel area" and a "single customs territory".[37] Conciliatory as it reads, this arrangement cannot resolve the problem of Northern Ireland of having to exit from the EU in law and not being able to leave it in reality without running the serious risk of reviving the old conflict.

D.   *A Blow to Union Citizenship*

Looking at the wording of the Founding Treaties alone, the effects of Brexit are probably limited to Article 52 TEU which defines their territorial scope and, to that end, enumerates the Member States. That the EU is not only a community of States, however, but also of its citizens has been one of its constitutive characteristics early on.[38] As the ECJ has repeatedly held, Union citizenship is "designed to be the fundamental status of nationals of the Member States".[39] This high tone complies with the polls in most EU states according to which a substantial majority of people subscribes to the concept of being "European".[40] Since the fact that the referendum is attributed largely

---

35   Northern Ireland Peace Agreement (The Good Friday Agreement) of 10 April 1998, available at https://peacemaker.un.org/sites/peacemaker.un.org/files/ IE% 20GB_980410_Northern%20Ireland%20Agreement.pdf.

36   Agreement between the Government of the United Kingdom of Great Britain and Northern Ireland and the Government of Ireland, found id. (above note 35), Preamble, para. 3.

37   Articles 4 to 6 of the Protocol on Ireland/Northern Ireland.

38   ECJ, *van Gend en Loos*, Case 26/62, [1963] ECR 1, pp. 12/13.

39   ECJ, *Grzelczyk*, Case C-184/99, [2001] ECR I-6229, para. 31.

40   European Commission, Standard Eurobarometer No. 89 (Spring 2018), p. 4.

to a wide-spread rejection among the British population against intra-EU migration,[41] the very concept of Union citizenship seems to be in question.

As far as specific needs of UK and EU citizens before and after Brexit are concerned, the immediate consequences obviously will depend on whether or not an arrangement like the Draft Withdrawal Agreement can be made. For both groups of citizens, their rights to residence is likely to be upheld, whereas acquired social rights are under peril in the event of a no-deal Brexit,[42] with no jurisdiction of a supranational judiciary that could safeguard legal protection.

The effect of Brexit on the concept of citizenship as such is at least equally significant, to say the least. In the wake the enlargement of the EU towards the East, the *Grzelczyk* jurisprudence, according to which the Member States owe mutual solidarity to EU citizens in distress,[43] has ceded under the Union citizen directive 2004/38[44] and its interpretation by the ECJ which allows Member States to exclude Unions citizens from other EU countries from most non-contributory social benefits.[45] How far this development is due to the willingness of citizens of poor EU countries to seek their place of residence where social security schemes seem favourable is a question for migration economy to answer. In any event, it has incrementally brought an end to an ideal, i.e. a European status of citizenship which likewise encompasses civil, political and social rights at EU level, as it was designed in the Maastricht Treaty of 1992 in what are today Articles 20 to 25 TFEU.[46] Brexit has not caused this change, but it fits with a general trend and probably marks its point of culmination. The vision of unrestricted free movement within Europe, apparently, has proved an overcharge to solidarity, and this holds true for both ends of the spectrum along which wealth is distributed in Europe. A possible and not unlikely reaction world be a further re-orientation of European citizenship towards the market freedoms. Considering the wide-spread critique of the EU as an actor with a neo-liberal agenda, such an outcome might seem paradoxical – and potentially self-destructive. Like a drop of ink in a glass of water, this spirit will continue to spread; at best, it will become thinner over time as it diffuses, but it cannot be filtered out anymore.

---

41 See the nuanced account by *Deakin*, Brexit, Labour Rights and Migration: Why Wisbech Matters to Brussels, GLJ 17 (2016) Brexit Supplement, 13 ff.

42 See the contribution by *Christoph Schewe* in this volume.

43 Above note 39.

44 OJ 2004 L 229/35.

45 ECJ, *Dano*, Case C-333/13, EU:C:2014:2358; *Alimanovic*, Case C-67/14, EU:C:2015:597; *Commission v UK*, Case C-308/14, EU:C:2016:436.

46 *Kadelbach*, Union Citizenship, in: *von Bogdandy and Bast* (eds.), Principles of European Constitutional Law, 2nd ed. 2010, 443, at 450 and 473 ff.

E. Future Relations between the European Union and the United Kingdom

At the time of writing, nobody knows whether, and if so, when and how Brexit will take place. However, since it is likely that Britain will leave the EU, some thought ought to be devoted to the possible nature of the future relationship between UK and the EU. The task is the more difficult as the political factions in Britain have yet to define their priorities for the orientation of an agreement that would deal with the matter. Some core issues, however, can be identified, and the joint EU/UK political declaration on the framework for future relationship takes note of them.[47]

To begin with, it is certain that the EU will not agree to any arrangement that would make Britain better off in terms of economic and financial advantages than it still is as a Member State of the EU. Therefore, it can be ruled out that the internal market between the two partners will stay as it is. On the other hand, it is very likely that both sides will suffer losses so that it is reasonable to retain rules and regulations which keep mutual trade in goods alive.

Secondly, it appears clear that other parts of the single market will not remain intact. While the EU is under an obligation to protect the rights of Union citizens who are already residents of the UK,[48] free movement of persons as it used to be will not be among the outcomes of the deal. This will come at a price, which is likely to be the freedom to provide financial services. The EU/UK political declaration on the framework for future relationship only very vaguely covers this sector;[49] it is expected that British banks will have to apply for licenses to access the single market in a complicated procedure, and the result promises little certainty for long-term activities.[50]

---

47   Political Declaration setting out the Framework for the Future Relationship between the European Union and the United Kingdom of 22 November 2018, https://assets.publishing.service.gov.uk/government/uploads/system/uploads/attachment_data/file/758556/22_November_Draft_Political_Declaration_setting _out_the_framework_for_the_future_relationship_between_the_EU_and_the _UK__agreed_at_negotiators__level_and_agreed_in_principle_at_political_ level__subject_to_endorsement_by_Leaders.pdf.

48   Cf. *Eeckhout and Frantziou*, (above note 9), at 718 ff.

49   Above note 47, pt. 38.

50   *Moloney*, Financial Services, the EU, and Brexit: An Uncertain Future for the City? GLJ 17 (2016) Brexit Supplement, 75 ff.; *id.*, Brexit and Financial Services: (Yet) Another Re-ordering of Institutional Governance for the EU Financial System? CML Rev. 55 (2018) Special Issue, 174, 179 f.

Thirdly, if British and European standards shall be held compatible, a mechanism for agreement on common rules must be put in place. This will necessitate common committees and/or reference to legal acts of the EU and, in this case, some kind of involvement of Britain in a law-making process if the rules referred to should be changed.

Finally, it is likely if not necessary that a dispute settlement procedure has to be set up, which raises the question of how the competent body relates to the integrity of EU law as it is required for arbitration in the realm of EU competencies by the ECJ.[51]

The final outcome, if achieved, will depend on political will. However, there are various designs of treaties in which the EU has engaged in the past that could serve as model types. All of them are association agreements as they are mentioned in Article 217 TFEU as an option for the EU to conclude treaties with third states. They rest on varying legal bases, including, but not exclusively, the common commercial policy power (Article 207 TFEU); since most of these treaties involve competencies still in the hands of the Member States, they are mostly so-called mixed agreements to which the EU as well as its Member States are parties.

To take EU relations with Turkey as a model type would mean to set up an association council with the task to enact further secondary law, such as on a customs union and regulated freedom of movement for persons.[52] Apart from the connotations triggered by the political system of Turkey and its growing distance to common European notions, the disadvantages of the EU/Turkey model is that many subject matters are excluded. Moreover, it is far from certain if a progressive development towards a customs union, which meanwhile forms an integral part of the model, could find sufficient political support in the UK.

A second model figures as "Norway" or "Norway plus", alluding to the fact that Norway entertains close relations with the EU in the framework of

---

51   ECJ, *Achmea*, Case C- 284/16, EU:C:2018:158, para. 39; pt. 134 of the joint declaration (above note 47) envisages reference to the CJEU if a question of interpretation of Union law should arise.

52   Based on the Agreement establishing an Association between the EEC and Turkey of 12 September 1963 and Additional Protocol of 23 November 1970, OJ 1973 C 113/1.

the European Economic Area (EEA),[53] but has expressed its distance to formal membership in the EU in referenda twice, in 1972 and 1994.[54] The advantage for Britain could be that a substantial part of EU law, such as on fair competition, consumer protection and environmental law, could be maintained in a proved pattern, whereas the principles of supremacy and direct effect would not apply. European citizenship could be converted into a stable post-Brexit status.[55] On the other hand, EEA is no political community, and the area of freedom, security and justice does not form part of it. What makes the EEA unattractive to British wishes to "regain control", however, is the very fact that freedom of movement is one of the areas of EEA law, that financing of some of the common policies is required, and that EEA Member States do not participate in EU legislation, but have to update domestic law to avoid suspensions of rights under the EEA Agreement; as for entry into, and amendments of, this treaty framework Britain would have to negotiate with the EU jointly with the other EEA states, which largely excludes desired outcomes that would apply individually to the UK alone.

What remains are treaties of the Canada (CETA) and of the Switzerland type. Whereas the free trade area with Canada rests on a single comprehensive treaty,[56] Switzerland has concluded a total of more than 120 agreements with the EU.[57] Relations of the Switzerland type allow it the parties to develop relations tailored specifically to the needs of individual partners and therefore appears to lend itself as a design a British/EU treaty could follow. However, such packages of detailed rules and regulations demand substantial efforts of negotiation, maintenance, updating, and quiet routine, which is unlikely to be invested by Britain in a foreseeable future. Therefore, it will be necessary that the EU take the initiative and does most of the drafting, which is much more realistic to accomplish in the framework of a single document of the Canada type. Thus, with a little help from EU, the British might get what many always wanted:[58] A common trade area with Europe, in company

---

53   Agreement on the European Economic Area, OJ 1994 L 1/3.

54   Cf. *Burke, Hannesson and Bangsund*, Schrödinger's Cake? Territorial Truths for Post-Brexit Britain, Neth. Yb. Int'l L. 47 (2016), 287, 301 ff.

55   Cf. *Kostakopoulou, Scala Civium*: Citizenship Templates Post-Brexit and the European Union's Duty to Protect EU Citizens, JCMS 2018, 1 ff., with a discussion of alternative scenarios.

56   Comprehensive Economic and Trade Agreement of 30 October 2016, OJ 2017 L 11/23.

57   See the contribution by *Astrid Epiney* and *Sian Affolter* in this volume.

58   *Judt* (above note 13), at 307 f.

with other countries of the Commonwealth such as Canada or India, Australia, and New Zealand, which have started to negotiate, or recently indicated interest of doing so, similar treaty relations with the European Union.[59]

---

59   Negotiations for a comprehensive trade agreement with India were started in 2007, but suspended in 2013; negotiations between the EU and Australia as well as with New Zealand were authorized by the Council on 22 May 2018, see http://ec.europa.eu/trade/policy/countries-and-regions/countries/.

Brexit: New Dawn Or Road To Perdition?

Anthony Arnull

A. Introduction

On 23 January 2013, the then British Prime Minister, *David Cameron*, gave a speech at the London offices of *Bloomberg*. The speech was about the future of Europe. In it *Cameron* announced that, at the next general election in 2015, he would seek a mandate from the British people to negotiate a new settlement with the 27 other Member States of the European Union (EU). Once it had been negotiated, it would be put to the British people in an in/out referendum: did they want to stay in the EU on the new terms that had been agreed or to come out altogether? Thus did *Cameron* fire the starting gun on a process that would eject him from office, divide the UK against itself and threaten economic and social calamity.

Cameron found himself on the losing side in the 2016 referendum and was replaced as Prime Minister on 13 July 2016 by *Theresa May*. Like *Cameron*, *May* was a remainer, albeit a rather unenthusiastic one. An outline of the new Prime Minister's approach to the forthcoming negotiations with the EU27 was given in her speech to the Conservative Party Conference on 2 October 2016. There the Prime Minister made it clear that Article 50 TEU would be triggered by the end of March 2017. She emphasised that she would be seeking an agreement that gave "British companies the maximum freedom to trade with and operate within the Single Market – and let European businesses do the same [in the UK]." She made it clear that leaving would mean regaining control of immigration (thus ruling out membership of the internal market or the European Economic Area) and removing the UK from the jurisdiction of the European Court of Justice (ECJ), which leavers had long regarded with suspicion as a "foreign" court.[1]

---

1   For critical commentary on the Court by UK authors, see e.g. *Hamson*, Methods of interpretation – A critical assessment of the results, in: ECJ (ed.), Judicial and Academic Conference, 27–28 September 1976, Reports, II-3 (II-10); *Neill*, The European Court of Justice: A Case Study in Judicial Activism, 1995; *Hartley*, The European Court, Judicial Objectivity and the Constitution of the European Union, Law Quarterly Review 112 (1996), 95. A case which attracted particular disapproval from eurosceptics was ECJ, *United Kingdom v Council*, Case C-84/94, [1996] ECR I-5755, which concerned the working time directive.

B. The Miller case

The Prime Minister's rhetoric at this point and the closeness of the result in the referendum – 51.9 % against 48.1 % – seemed to polarise the country and foster an atmosphere of intolerance. This was evident in the climate that surrounded the legal challenge brought by *Gina Miller*, a businesswoman, to the government's intention to notify the EU of the UK's intention to withdraw without legislative authorisation by Parliament.

The decision of the High Court that such authorisation was required led a mass-market tabloid newspaper to denounce the judges involved as "enemies of the people". When the case reached the United Kingdom Supreme Court (UKSC), its President, *Lord Neuberger*, began his judgment by explaining why it was appropriate for the courts to determine the issue at stake and that the case had nothing to do with the wisdom of the decision to withdraw from the EU. In the event, the UKSC upheld the decision of the High Court and confirmed that an Act of Parliament was needed to give the government authority to notify the European Council of the UK's decision.[2]

The *Miller* case presented the Supreme Court with an opportunity to consider the much-debated question whether notification by a Member State under Article 50 TEU of its intention to withdraw from the EU could be revoked. The view that revocation is legally possible is perhaps more widely held in the UK than in the EU27. Politically, however, there have been signs that such a move by the UK would not be resisted by the EU27.

In *Miller*, the parties were agreed that notification under Article 50 TEU could not be withdrawn. The majority stated:

> "[...] we are content to proceed on the basis that that is correct, without expressing any view of our own [...]. It follows from this that once the United Kingdom gives Notice, it will inevitably cease at a later date to be a member of the European Union and a party to the EU Treaties."[3]

Both parties were keen to avoid a reference to the ECJ on the matter. If it turned out that notice under Article 50 TEU was revocable, the government would have faced the prospect of constant harrying about the progress of the negotiations and calls for them to be halted or suspended. For the applicants, their argument that invoking Article 50 TEU would necessarily mean the end of EU rights in the UK would have been undermined. So the UKSC dealt with the case on the basis of an assumption about the legal position which it knew might be incorrect but without deciding one way or the other what the

---

2   *R (Miller) v Secretary of State* [2017] UKSC 5.
3   Ibid., para. 26.

correct legal position was. A reference could have resolved the matter. However, as a matter of judicial politics, the idea of involving in a primarily domestic dispute an institution of the very organisation the UK wished to leave must have seemed very unattractive.

It was not until 3 October 2018 that a British court referred to the ECJ the question whether a notification given under Article 50 TEU might be revoked. That question was posed by the Court of Session, Inner House, First Division (Scotland) in *Wightman and Others v Secretary of State for Exiting the European Union,*[4] in which the applicants included members of the Scottish, UK and European Parliaments. The question itself was accompanied by a request that the case be dealt with under the expedited procedure provided for in Article 105(1) of the Court's Rules of Procedure, a request to which the President of the Court acceded by Order dated 19 October 2018.[5]

It is understood that an application by the government to the referring court to have the reference suspended was unsuccessful. The government subsequently applied for permission to appeal to the UKSC, but that application was not scheduled to be heard until shortly before the hearing of the case before the ECJ. This placed the government's attempt to prevent the ECJ from ruling on the case in some difficulty, particularly in view of the limits imposed in the *Cartesio* case[6] on the right to appeal against a reference for a preliminary ruling. That case effectively made judgments of superior courts on the appropriateness of a reference by a lower court merely advisory where the case remained pending before the latter court.[7]

The President's Order suggests that the Court intends to take the opportunity presented by the reference to rule on the matter. According to the Order,

> "[…] the referring court sets out grounds that undeniably indicate that there is a need to make a ruling urgently. In particular, as is stated in the order for reference, it is necessary to clarify the scope of Article 50 TEU before the Members of the national

---

4   *Wightman and Others v Secretary of State for Exiting the European Union* [2018] CSIH 62.
5   ECJ, *Wightman and Others*, Case C-621/18, EU:C:2018:851.
6   ECJ, *Cartesio*, Case C-210/06, [2008] ECR I-9641.
7   See *Broberg/Fenger*, Preliminary References to the European Court of Justice, 2nd ed., 2014, pp. 329-330; *Broberg/Fenger*, Preliminary references as a right: but for whom? The extent to which preliminary reference decisions can be subject to appeal, European Law Review 36 (2011), 276.

Parliament make a decision on the withdrawal agreement, referred to in that article, which might be submitted to them."[8]

The Order went on to describe Article 50 TEU as "of fundamental importance for the United Kingdom and for the constitutional order of the European Union [...]."[9]

What is less clear is how the Court will rule on the substance of the case. On the one hand, a Member State which has notified the EU of its intention to withdraw pursuant to Article 50 TEU might change its mind, for example, if there was a change of government. Any deal ultimately reached might be rejected by the national legislature of the State concerned or by its people in a referendum. These outcomes might be regarded as revoking the original decision to withdraw, which might in turn be seen as invalidating all subsequent steps in the procedure that had been taken.

On the other hand, permitting a Member State to withdraw a notification under Article 50 TEU might allow the process to be used to extract political concessions by a State which had no real intention to withdraw. Moreover, it is not clear what the process would be for withdrawing a notification. Would it be a unilateral act of the State concerned or would it require the consent of the other Member States? If the latter, would they decide by qualified majority or would unanimity be necessary? It is not difficult to imagine a situation in which the remaining Member States had come to the conclusion that they would be better off without the departing State.[10]

C.   The Article 50 TEU letter

Parliament subsequently passed the European Union (Notification of Withdrawal) Act 2017 to give effect to the UKSC's ruling in *Miller*. This enabled the Prime Minister to write to the President of the European Council, *Donald Tusk*, on 29 March 2017 to inform him of the UK's intention to withdraw from the European Union. The letter was, however, a blunder.

It was well known that the *Cameron* government had not made any preparations for a leave vote before the referendum for fear that, if it did, the news

---

8   Order of the President of the ECJ, *Wightman and Others*, Case C-621/18, EU:C:2018:851, para. 9.

9   Ibid., para. 11.

10   For more discussion of these issues, see *Craig*, Brexit: A Drama in Six Acts, European Law Review 41 (2016), 447 (463 ff.); *Eeckhout/Fantziou*, Brexit and Article 50: A Constitutionalist Reading, Common Market Law Review 54 (2017), 695 (711 ff.); *Sari*, Reversing a Withdrawal Notification under Article 50 TEU: Can a Member State Change its Mind?, European Law Review 42 (2017), 451.

would leak out and undermine the remain campaign. We now know that the *May* government had not conducted any serious study of the real-world effects of leaving the EU before the fateful letter was dispatched to *Donald Tusk*. Nor did the government at that point have any clear view of what it was seeking to achieve in the negotiations. These fundamental issues all had to be resolved with the Article 50 TEU clock ticking ever more loudly in the background.

So why did the Prime Minister surrender so cheaply the one aspect of the Article 50 TEU procedure she had the power to control? The short answer is that she had promised to trigger Article 50 TEU by the end of March 2017. But why did she make that promise? Like her predecessor, she seems to have been motivated by party political considerations. Some in her party thought that the UK should ignore Article 50 TEU and just walk away. Some thought that the passions raised by the referendum were so powerful that the process needed to be started and finished as soon as possible. But the Prime Minister had just won a leadership contest. She was in the ascendant. She had a reputation for careful attention to detail. She should not have triggered Article 50 TEU before the UK was ready to lock horns with the EU27.

D.   *The European Union (Withdrawal) Bill*

In her speech to the party conference, the Prime Minister also announced that the government would bring forward a bill to repeal the European Communities Act 1972 (ECA). This is the act that provides the legal basis for the application of EU law in the UK. The bill, formally entitled the European Union (Withdrawal) Bill, was introduced on 13 July 2017. It eventually became law on 26 June 2018 as the European Union (Withdrawal) Act (EUWA).

The explanatory notes published when the bill was originally introduced give a good summary of the effect of the Act:

> "The Bill ends the supremacy of European Union (EU) law in UK law and converts EU law as it stands at the moment of exit into domestic law. It also creates temporary powers to make secondary legislation to enable corrections to be made to the laws that would otherwise no longer operate appropriately once the UK has left, so that the domestic legal system continues to function correctly outside the EU. The Bill

also enables domestic law to reflect the content of a withdrawal agreement under Article 50 of the Treaty on European Union once the UK leaves the EU."[11]

One of the principal innovations of the Act is to create a new category of domestic law called "retained EU law", which is anything which continues to be part of domestic law by virtue of the Act (section 6(7)). It may take a number of forms. "EU-derived domestic legislation" (section 2) will include legislation adopted under section 2(2) of the ECA to give effect to EU directives. "Direct EU legislation" (section 3) includes EU regulations, which would have been directly applicable and therefore not have required any national measures of implementation. The Act also converts directly effective provisions of the Treaties into national law (section 4). It is expressly stated that the Charter of Fundamental Rights will not form part of UK domestic law post Brexit (section 5(4)).

Section 6(3) and (4) of the Withdrawal Act effectively give judgments of the ECJ delivered before Brexit day the same status in national law as judgments of the UKSC. Under section 6(2), any national court or tribunal may have regard to a judgment of the ECJ delivered after Brexit day "so far as it is relevant to any matter before the court or tribunal." In addition, it may be noted that Article 82 of the draft Withdrawal Agreement published by the Commission on 19 March 2018 provides that the ECJ would continue to have jurisdiction over direct actions involving the UK and preliminary rulings sought by UK courts until the end of the transitional period for which the draft Agreement provides. So the Court may retain an important residual influence on the law applicable in the UK beyond 29 March 2019. The position after the end of the transitional period will depend on whether an agreement on the future relationship between the UK and the EU has been agreed by then and, if so, what it says.

The Withdrawal Act gives ministers powers to deal with "deficiencies arising from withdrawal" (section 8(1)). An example of a "deficiency" would be where retained EU law "has no practical application in relation to the United Kingdom or is otherwise redundant" (section 8(2)(a)) or confers functions on EU entities which no longer have jurisdiction in any part of the UK (section 8(2)(b)).

Section 8(5) provides: "Regulations under subsection (1) may make any provision that could be made by Act of Parliament." This is an example of what is known as a *Henry VIII* clause: within its scope, it gives ministers the power to do anything that Parliament could do. The relevant clause attracted

---

11   European Union (Withdrawal) Bill, Explanatory Note, https://publications.parliament.uk/pa/bills/cbill/2017-2019/0005/en/18005en.pdf, p. 4, last accessed 2 February 2019.

much criticism during the passage of the Bill through Parliament. The use of section 8 has therefore been made subject to certain restrictions of both substance and procedure. Section 8 may in any event only be used within two years of Brexit (section 8(8)).

The EUWA is the first of a series of Brexit-related Acts that will be needed.[12] If there is a Withdrawal Agreement (which cannot yet be taken for granted), there will be an EU (Withdrawal Agreement) Act to give effect to it in domestic law. The Withdrawal Agreement Bill will be introduced only once Parliament has approved the final deal in accordance with section 13 of the EUWA and will have to pass before the UK leaves the EU on 29 March 2019 so that the Withdrawal Agreement can enter into force immediately.[13]

E.   The 2017 general election and the start of the negotiations

It was widely recognised from the outset that the two-year deadline laid down in Article 50 TEU posed a significant challenge, particularly to the departing state. One might therefore have expected the UK government to make full use of the negotiating period. But on 18 April 2017 the Prime Minister announced that she wished to hold a general election in the hope of increasing her majority in Parliament. People were quick to point out that, if an election were necessary, it would have been better to hold it before triggering Article 50 TEU rather than afterwards.

In the event, a poor campaign saw the government's majority of 17 wiped out in the election held on 8 June 2017. It had to come to an agreement with the ten Members of Parliament of the Democratic Unionist Party in order to govern. The Prime Minister emerged from the election a significantly weakened figure, unable to control her cabinet or party.

The general election meant that the negotiations did not start until 19 June 2017, when the UK immediately abandoned its insistence that the Withdrawal Agreement should be negotiated alongside its future relationship with the EU27 and accepted their phased approach. Other than that, four days of talks were devoted mainly to house-keeping arrangements. Issues of substance were considered for the first time when talks resumed on 17 July. By

---

12   There will also be a Customs Act, a Trade Act and an Immigration Act (plus acts on fisheries, agriculture, nuclear safety (resulting from the UK's withdrawal from Euratom) and international sanctions).

13   See *Department for Exiting the European Union*, Legislating for the Withdrawal Agreement between the United Kingdom and the European Union, Cm 9674, July 2018.

that stage the EU had published more than 20 so-called position papers. By contrast, the UK government had published just two white papers and four position papers.

Why was the UK so poorly prepared for the start of the negotiations? The gung-ho approach of the Brexiters, some of whom sat in the cabinet, may have led them to underestimate the scale of the task. Some, including the Prime Minister herself ("no deal is better than a bad deal"), seemed sanguine about the prospect of no agreement being reached, although it now seems to be widely recognised that the absence of a deal would be calamitous for the UK (and damaging to other Member States too).

There is no doubt that things did not start well. UK proposals on citizens' rights which it described as generous turned out to be less advantageous than those put forward by the EU. UK proposals for avoiding a hard border between Northern Ireland and the Irish Republic were described by an EU official as "magical thinking". Progress on the size of the divorce bill and the way it might be calculated was slow.

F.   The Florence speech and movement to the second phase

In an attempt to jump-start the negotiations, the Prime Minister travelled to Florence, Italy, where she gave a speech on 22 September 2017. The Prime Minister reassured the EU27 that there was no need for them "to fear that they will need to pay more or receive less over the remainder of the current budget plan [...]. The United Kingdom will honour commitments we have made during the period of our membership." The UK wished to continue "to take part in those specific policies and programmes [...] that promote science, education and culture – and those that promote our mutual security" and would "make an ongoing contribution to cover our fair share of the costs involved."

The speech was well received in Europe, but the fourth (25-28 September 2017) and fifth (9-12 October 2017) rounds of negotiations failed to produce the breakthrough that had been hoped for. At the meeting of the European Council on 19-20 October 2017, the EU27 considered that insufficient progress had been made to justify moving to the second phase of the negotiations. Ireland was growing increasingly concerned about the lack of concrete and practical proposals from the UK about how a hard border with the north would be avoided. Because it effectively had a veto over any decision to move to the second stage of the negotiations, it announced that it would not agree to that step being taken until the UK tabled serious proposals.

In the course of a frantic week of shuttle diplomacy in early December 2017, the Prime Minister succeeded in getting agreement on a border text that commanded the support of all parties. On Friday 8 December, she and *Jean-Claude Juncker*, the President of the European Commission, held a press conference at which they announced that sufficient progress had been made. The content of the agreement that had been reached was published on the same day as a "Joint report from the negotiators […] on progress during phase 1 […]." The Joint Report was accompanied by a communication from the Commission on the state of progress of the negotiations[14] in which it recommended to the European Council that it should find sufficient progress to have been made to allow the second phase of the negotiations to begin. That recommendation was accepted by the European Council on 15 December 2017.

The European Council agreed to negotiate a transitional period with the UK, pointing out that the UK, as a third country, would cease to participate in EU institutions and decision-making. The transitional arrangements would be set out in the Withdrawal Agreement and would require the UK to accept all Union rules (including the four freedoms) as well as the jurisdiction of the ECJ. They would require the UK to remain in the EU Customs Union and the single market, which would prevent it from implementing new trade agreements with third countries. This would be politically and symbolically difficult for the UK, though it would have little practical effect, particularly as the UK would be free to negotiate with third countries, because such agreements are likely to take much longer to agree than the two years or so for which the transitional period was expected to last.

G.   *The Chequers Agreement*

Almost since the start of the negotiations, the EU27 had been asking the UK to set out what it was hoping to achieve. Beyond the rather general terms of the Prime Minister's speeches, however, little had been forthcoming. This was largely due to divergent views within the cabinet on what Brexit should look like. The Prime Minister attempted to break the deadlock in a meeting at Chequers, her country retreat, on 6 July 2018. The outcome of the meeting was set out in a Statement from HM Government issued when the meeting

---

14   Communication from the Commission to the European Council (Article 50) on the state of progress of the negotiations with the United Kingdom under Article 50 of the Treaty on European Union, COM(2017) 784 final of 8 December 2017.

finished with further detail being supplied in a White Paper entitled "The Future Relationship between the United Kingdom and the European Union"[15] published shortly thereafter.

The Statement began by reiterating that the UK would leave the EU on 29 March 2019. It then declared: "After a time-limited implementation period that will conclude at the end of 2020, the UK and the EU will enter into a new relationship – one that must work for both sides [...]."[16] This was interesting because it confirmed the government's determination to conclude an agreement on the UK's future relationship with the EU in time for it to enter into force at the end of the transition period. It had originally been thought in some quarters that the agreement on the future relationship would take much longer to conclude and that there might be a gap between the end of the transition period and the entry into force of the agreement, when WTO rules would presumably apply. This was a highly unattractive prospect because it would mean that businesses would have to adapt twice, once at the end of the transition period and again when the agreement on the future relationship (assuming one could be reached) entered into force.

The blueprint agreed by the government had a number of elements.
-   The UK and the EU would maintain common rules for goods, with the UK committing to ongoing harmonisation with EU rules on goods where necessary to provide frictionless trade at the border.
-   Different arrangements would be made for services to ensure regulatory flexibility, it being recognised that the UK and the EU would not have current levels of access to each other's markets.
-   The legal agreements setting out the future relationship would contain strong reciprocal commitments to open and fair trade. The UK would apply "a common rulebook on state aid" and establish "co-operative arrangements between regulators on competition." The UK and the EU would agree to "maintain high regulatory standards for the environment, climate change, social and employment [sic], and consumer protection [...]."
-   "The UK and the EU would establish a joint institutional framework to provide for the consistent interpretation and application of UK-EU agreements by both parties."
-   "The UK and the EU would work together on the phased introduction of a new Facilitated Customs Arrangement that would remove

---

15   *Department for Exiting the European Union*, The future relationship between the United Kingdom and the European Union, Cm 9593, July 2018.
16   The UK government prefers "implementation period" to "transition period". The draft Withdrawal Agreement sanctions the use of either term: see Art 121. The latter seems more appropriate.

the need for customs checks and controls between the UK and the
EU as if a combined customs territory."

The final two elements of the blueprint require elaboration.

On consistent interpretation and application, the government explained
that "[t]his would be done in the UK by UK courts, and in the EU by EU
courts – with due regard paid to EU case law in areas where the UK continued
to apply a common rulebook." The framework would also include "robust
and appropriate means for the resolution of disputes, including through a
Joint Committee and in many areas through binding independent arbitration
– accommodating through a joint reference procedure the role of the Court
of Justice of the European Union (CJEU) as the interpreter of EU rules, but
founded on the principle that the court of one party cannot resolve disputes
between the two."[17]

Under the "Facilitated Customs Arrangement", "[t]he UK would apply the
UK's tariffs and trade policy for goods intended for the UK, and the EU's
tariffs and trade policy for goods intended for the EU [...]. This would enable
the UK to control its own tariffs for trade with the rest of the world and ensure
businesses paid the right or no tariff – in the vast majority of cases upfront,
and otherwise through a repayment mechanism."[18] The government argued
that such a relationship would enable the UK and the EU to meet their commitments to Northern Ireland and Ireland and allow remaining Withdrawal
Agreement issues to be resolved.

The *Chequers deal* was unanimously endorsed by the cabinet on 6 July
2018. However, two days later on 8 July *David Davis*, the then Brexit Secretary, resigned claiming that current policy would make it more difficult "to
deliver on the mandate of the referendum, and on our manifesto commitment
to leave the Customs Union and the Single Market." He was replaced by
Dominic Raab, another leaver. On 9 July, the Foreign Secretary, *Boris Johnson*, also resigned, claiming that the Brexit dream was dying and that Britain
risked becoming a "colony" of the EU. *Johnson* was replaced by *Jeremy
Hunt*, a remainer.

Amid rumours of disquiet about the *Chequers Agreement* among grass-
roots Tories, EU Chief Negotiator *Michel Barnier* rejected it, saying that the
EU would not delegate the application of its law to a non-member country.
One especially thorny issue is the so-called backstop solution for avoiding a
hard border in Northern Ireland. This would involve Northern Ireland staying
in a customs union and single market for goods post Brexit. Brexiters dislike
this idea because they regard it as effectively creating a border in the Irish

---

17   *Department for Exiting the European Union*, (note 15), p. 11.
18   Statement from HM Government, Chequers, 6 July 2018, para. 4(d).

Sea and requiring trade between Northern Ireland and the rest of the UK to take place on different terms to trade between, say, Scotland and England.

In August 2018, the government began to issue a series of so-called technical notices offering advice on steps that might usefully be taken to prepare for a no-deal Brexit. The general message of the notices was that the consequences of a no-deal Brexit, in which the UK left the EU abruptly on 29 March 2019 with no transitional period and little time in which to prepare, would be disastrous.[19]

H. The end of part one?

At the time of writing, much still hangs in the balance.

At a meeting in Salzburg, Austria, on 20 September 2018, the Prime Minister presented her *Chequers plan* to the Heads of State or Government of the EU27. The mood music in the run-up to the summit had led her to expect some words of encouragement. However, the UK made a series of gaffes. *Liam Fox*, the International Trade Secretary, announced ahead of the summit that he wanted to repeal a large quantity of health standards to facilitate a trade deal with the USA. The Prime Minister informed *Leo Varadkar*, the Irish Prime Minister, on the morning of the summit that there was unlikely to be a solution to the Irish border issue in time for the October 17 summit, at which it had been hoped the Withdrawal Agreement might in principle be agreed. In the 10-minute after-dinner speech the Prime Minister had been allowed to give, she antagonised her audience by adopting a belligerent tone and reading from an article she had published the previous day in a German newspaper.

All this soured the mood and the EU27 responded by saying that *Chequers* was unworkable and did not offer a way forward. This was interpreted by the British press as a humiliation for the Prime Minister, who gave a speech the following day demanding respect. This she was accorded at the October 2018 summit, though hopes that the EU27 would agree on that occasion to reconvene in November 2018 to finalise the Withdrawal Agreement were dashed when it became clear that the issue of the Irish border had yet to be resolved.

The atmosphere in which the Prime Minister was operating at home was even more febrile than had become the norm as speculation grew that the UK would end up having to leave the EU on 29 March 2019 without a deal. At

---

19   See https://www.gov.uk/government/publications/uk-governments-preparations-for-a-no-deal-scenario, last accessed 2 February 2019.

the same time, the Prime Minister began to flirt with the idea that the transitional period envisaged by the draft Withdrawal Agreement might be extended to allow more time for the future relationship to be agreed. Interestingly, she did not suggest an extension to the negotiating period pursuant to Article 50(3) TEU even though this might have given the UK greater leverage by preserving its status as a Member State. Presumably the Prime Minister calculated that this would be too much for her party to bear, though many of her colleagues were distinctly unimpressed by her proposal to extend the transitional period.

Optimists hope that the Withdrawal Agreement and a political declaration outlining the UK's future relationship with the EU will be agreed at a summit pencilled in for 17-18 November. This is regarded as the latest practical date on which the Agreement could be finalised. The reason is that it will then have to be agreed by the UK Parliament under section 13 of the EUWA (not necessarily a forgone conclusion) and the EU (Withdrawal Agreement) Bill will have to have reached the statute book. It will also have to be approved by the European Parliament and the Council (acting by qualified majority) in accordance with Article 50(2) TEU. Choreographing all this will not be an easy task: section 13(2) EUWA says that as far as practicable the Withdrawal Agreement must be voted on by the House of Commons before the European Parliament does so.

Section 13 EUWA also makes provision for what will happen if the Withdrawal Agreement fails to secure the approval of the House of Commons. This will essentially involve a process of dialogue between the House of Commons and the government over what to do next. This could result in: (a) the government returning to the negotiating table or even seeking an extension of the negotiating deadline in accordance with Article 50 TEU (though the government has so far ruled this out); (b) the UK leaving without a deal; (c) a snap General Election and a new government, which might seek an extension of the negotiating period or hold a further referendum if this is feasible within the time available.

If the Withdrawal Agreement is rejected by the European Parliament or there is no qualified majority in its support in the Council, the ball will be in the court of the EU, though the UK can be expected to makes its voice heard, especially if the Agreement has been approved by the House of Commons. The options available may depend on whether the Agreement has been rejected by: (a) the European Parliament alone; (b) a single Member State (and which one); (c) the European Parliament and a single Member State (and which one); (d) multiple Member States (and which ones); (e) multiple Member States and the European Parliament.

If the Agreement has been rejected by the European Parliament and several large Member States, that may mean that the UK has to leave without a deal, although it may still be possible to agree ad hoc arrangements to resolve particular issues. If it has been rejected by the European Parliament alone or by the European Parliament and one or two small Member States, and provided the deadline of 29 March 2019 has not yet passed, the negotiating period might still be extended. The issue or issues that have caused the Agreement to be rejected will obviously also be relevant.

Meanwhile some people are continuing to campaign for Brexit to be halted. On 20 October 2018, an estimated 700,000 people took part in a demonstration in central London to demand a so-called "people's vote" on any Brexit deal agreed by the government. If Brexit happens, it is likely to please no-one. What seems certain is that it will harm everyone, but some more than others.

How will the EU Develop without the United Kingdom?

*Matthias Ruffert**

A.   *Introduction*

In the beginning, I wish to be very clear: This contribution and the whole symposium are consequential upon one of the most irresponsible political decisions in a European country in the last at least 50 years. After *Paul Craig's* seminal article on how Brexit came about,[1] it is not necessary to repeat the amateurish character of *David Cameron's* politics – let him hum to himself and leave number 10 Downing Street forever.[2] Likewise, it is certainly not worth spending our time on *Boris Johnson* and his relationship towards a cake – he probably ate it more than once and struggles with the consequences. But is it not irresponsible to the extreme to call into question the European identity of the United Kingdom? Our British friends should please correct me if my observation was wrong, but I have the impression that the parochialism expressed in the Brexit vote could, from the point of view of the Brexiteers, be disguised by a certain feeling of cultural dominance which was nothing more than a continuous loss of interest in 'continental' languages and cultures – these being matters for the "others" such as the Royal Family (just to think about the Prince of Wales' impeccable German). Maybe I am too pessimistic, and if so, the better, but I fear that Brexit contains the germ of unsurmountable obstacles for mutual understanding and cooperative togetherness. What this means for the UK is a matter for the other contributions, so I will stop at this point except one thing: Will future organisers of German conferences continue to be polite and arrange the whole debate in English so that everyone can follow (including instructions for transport and travel) – not only the EU citizens from Ireland, Malta and Cyprus? I hope so, if only to show that my efforts to struggle with your language

---

*   This is the version as presented orally in Frankfurt on 15 March 2018 with minor modifications. Parts of it were later published in German: *Ruffert*, Brexit – oder die Kunst harmonischer Desintegration, JZ 2018, 1005.
1   *Craig*, Brexit: A drama in six acts, EL Rev. 41 (2016), 447.
2   BBC-recording:https://www.youtube.com/watch?v=-Gz6mZYxS0A, last accessed 7 February 2019, like all online material cited in this contribution.

for now more than 41 years were not vain.[3] Please bear with it for the time being. But what a potential (and likely?) loss – for us 'continental Europeans'![4] Will *Handel's* music be a foreigner's from now on (as Microsoft word already suggests in not accepting the *Umlaut*)? Will the British never learn from us Germans that we have the obsession to watch *Freddie Frinton's* 'Dinner for One' on New Year's Eve? More seriously: Will we be cut off top British universities after the transition period? These reflections only cause – deep sadness.

The current British government's answer would of course be: "We are leaving the EU, not Europe!"[5] Or, in Prime Minister *Theresa May's* words of 2 March 2018: Brexit "… was not a vote for a distant relationship with our neighbours."[6] Oh yes, it was! Whoever claims the opposite, lives a lie, a lie that pretends to ensure survival of a particular view of national identity. Leaving the EU in 2017/2019 after a membership of more than 40 years is leaving Europe. This is a loss for Europe. Why it is a loss for Europe will be explained in two parts: first, with respect to particular British contribution to the EU and second, concerning the EU as a whole. Believe me: Some very uncomfortable things will have to be said towards the EU under both aspects.

B.   *The Loss of a Market-Oriented, Competitive, Anglo-American Partner*

I.   The UK as a Partner – and Policy Alternatives

Whom do we lose? Today, the United Kingdom represents roughly 13 % of the EU's population, about 15 % of its economic output and the largest banking industry. The public expenditure quota, which is on the lower side of the European schedule, is decreasing and lower than in Germany (44.7 %),

---

3   On the language issue cf. *Ruffert*, Remarks on the language of administrative law scholarship in the EU, Harlow, Leino and della Cananea (eds.), Research Handbook on EU Administrative Law, 2017, p. 69.

4   *van Middelaar*, Brexit as the European Union's „Machiavellian Moment", CMLRev. 55 (2018), 3, 6, mentions "from Shakespeare to Parliament to the Beatles".

5   Speech of Prime Minister *Theresa May* of 22 September 2017 in Florence (available at: https://www.gov.uk/government/speeches/pms-florence-speech-a-new-era-of-cooperation-and-partnership-between-the-uk-and-the-eu): „We may be leaving the European Union, but we are not leaving Europe."

6   Available at: https://www.gov.uk/government/speeches/pm-speech-on-our-future-economic-partnership-with-the-european-union.

around 41.3 %, compared to 55.9 % in France. Its unemployment rate is below 5 %.[7] Although the competitiveness of the British economy as a whole might give reason to doubts, there is no tendency to overcome negative developments by government spending or even nationalisation. In the spectrum of what is often called "varieties of capitalism", the UK is on the liberal side since the early 1980s. Let me quote Prime Minister *May* again: "… we share the same set of fundamental beliefs; a belief in free trade, rigorous and fair competition, strong consumer rights, and that trying to beat other countries' industries by unfairly subsidising one's own is a serious mistake."[8]

If we reflect upon what these figures and statements mean, we have to consider what the core of European integration and European law is above all. If there was agreement on the answer to this question, many of the current problems in the EU would not exist. Of course, there is no such agreement beyond the statement that the EU has been a guarantor of peace within Europe since the 1950s. Even this consensus has been challenged recently, on the basis that it was supposed to be the cold war that forced the old enemies in Western Europe to co-operate and not the foundation of the European Communities that brought long lasting peace to Europe. It is true that the influence of the Soviet threat cannot be denied – younger readers will get an idea of the pre-1989 atmosphere when listening to *Wladimir Putin's* speeches on nuclear weapons, and the generation which precedes mine has a strong collective memory of stockpiling food in the Cuban crisis. However, I would strongly advocate against diminishing the achievement of reconciliation in Central and Western Europe, and it is this peacebuilding achievement that Prime Minister *May* alludes to when reiterating the spell "We do not leave Europe!" This, at least is a good thing.

But what is the core of the European project beyond peace? The controversy about the answer could be depicted in a differentiated way, but we can also simplify it: Either, we are putting the emphasis on substantive economic policy, and law, or on institution building and the concomitant legal requirements.

In terms of substantive economic policy, the EU is a success story – also for the United Kingdom. The completion of the internal market is one of the greatest achievements in European history. There are still deficits, challenges to be taken, in the services sector in particular. But generally speaking, the

---

7   Figures on population and employment taken from Eurostat (http://ec.europa.eu/eurostat/de/home), on public expenditure from the Monatsbericht of the German Ministerium der Finanzen 10/2017.

8   Florence speech of *Theresa May*, note 5.

advantages of the internal market cannot easily be talked to death. The internal market is corroborated by a very strong competition law which imposes at least some market discipline upon global players, but also on the economic activity of the Member States. There is no better place than Frankfurt am Main to remind us of this context – *Franz Böhm,* who taught here and who succeeded *Walter Hallstein* as Rector of the Goethe-University in 1948, is one of the founding fathers of modern competition law in Europe.[9]

We know from history that there was always a strong interest in making the UK join the then European Economic Community, as it was in favour of integrated markets and fair competition. We also know from history that this economy based view is not the only perspective on European integration. And we know it from law: The chapter on the Common Agricultural Policy (CAP), today Articles 38 to 44 TFEU, are part of a historical compromise between France and Germany – opening the markets for industrial production here, strong agricultural policy there. I quote from Article 42 TFEU: "The provisions of the Chapter relating to rules on competition shall apply to production of and trade in agricultural products only to the extent determined by the European Parliament and the Council ..., account being taken of the objectives set out in Article 39.", the latter article describing the aims of the CAP. Today's Article 106 TFEU mirrors another important compromise, submitting public undertakings under the rules of competition law and the internal market in its first paragraph and formulating, in the second paragraph, an exception for "undertakings entrusted with the operation of services of general economic interest", the well-known French *service public.* There was a real risk of the latter compromise suffering a considerable imbalance when today's Article 14 TFEU on services of general interest was inserted into the Treaty of Amsterdam (1999) upon French pressure, further backed by Article 36 of the Fundamental Right's Charter, and when French President *Nicolas Sarkozy* tried to eliminate free competition from the aims of the Union in the negotiations preceding the signature of the Treaty of Lisbon (2007/2009); he failed, because the aim was preserved in a protocol of the same level as the Treaty.[10]

---

9   On *Böhm*'s concept see the recent paper by *Mohr*, Die Interdependenz der Ordnungen als rechts- und wirtschaftsphilosophische Konzeption, Juristenzeitung 73 (2018), 685, 692 ff.; *Voet van Vormizeele*, Kartellrecht und Verfassungsrecht, Neue Zeitschrift für Kartellrecht 1 (2013), 386, 390.

10   See the critical assessment by *Kotzur*, Die Soziale Marktwirtschaft nach dem Reformvertrag, in: Pernice (ed.), Der Vertrag von Lissabon: Reform der EU ohne Verfassung?, 2008, p. 197, 197 f.

In all these negotiations, the UK would rather side a market-oriented approach. It is possible, if not likely, that the EU will change following the British exit and become more State economy oriented. Some observers such as the German economist *Hans-Werner Sinn* are warning that the UK should be kept in the internal market as far as possible to avoid such effects.[11] This may be exaggerated, but it suffices to read the speech held by the Dutch Prime Minister *Mark Rutte* in Berlin in the beginning of this month to see where the lines of conflict are.[12] *Rutte* has a very co-operation-oriented view of Europe with a sceptical view on supranationalism. But he also underlines market orientation and stability. The problem is that the Netherlands are four times smaller in population than the UK and three times smaller in economic output (absolute figures).

The French, some say Mediterranean, approach needs a lot more institutional density, more complicated institution building. Redistributive policies have a stronger need for democratic legitimacy. It is doubtful whether this can be reached in the current state of European politics. It is certainly not helpful to lose an election and declare the United States of Europe – threatening exclusion to those who do not wish to participate. A lesson from Brexit that can be learnt for the future development of the EU is to keep the constitution, above all the economic constitution open for political debate and change. Changing majorities warrant enduring democracy. *Jean-Claude Juncker's* European Commission is the first to declare itself a political Commission; we know that Britain was explicitly opposing this very candidate. A political Commission at one time certainly does not have a mandate for making irreversible policy decisions.

II.   The 'Cherry-Picking' Question

If it is fair to say that British membership is an advantage for the EU – and I insist that this is true – would it not be fair as well to keep the UK as far in the EU as possible? This is often argued from an economist's point of view, and also by relevant interest groups – see only the recent calculation by the

---

11   *Sinn*, Brexit, Deutschland und die Zukunft der EU, Frankfurter Allgemeine Zeitung, Nr. 46, 23 February 2018, p. 20.

12   Speech of the *Dutch Prime Minister Mark Rutte*, Bertelsmann-Foundation, Berlin, 2 March 2018, available at: https://www.government.nl/documents/ speeches/2018/03/02/rede-des-niederlandischen-ministerprasidenten-mark-rutte -bertelsmann-stiftung-berlin.

Federation of German Industries (BDI)[13]. Some commentators are accusing the EU of negotiating with an intention to punish the British because of their negative referendum. Some even insinuate that *Michel Barnier* as a French would have such an attitude.

Of course, I never met *Michel Barnier,* and it is unlikely that he will ever tell us what his thoughts are when negotiating with *David Davies.* But I would submit that the position not to negotiate parts of the internal market has an inherent legal logic and is not to be seen as a measure of punishment. Legally, the internal market and competition law are in fact a comprehensive whole. Article 3, section 3, 1st sentence TEU could not be clearer: "The Union shall establish an internal market."[14] The internal market is further defined in Article 26 section 2 TFEU as: "The internal market shall comprise an area without internal frontiers in which the free movement of goods, persons, services and capital is ensured in accordance with the provisions of the Treaties." To cut out one of the economic goods enumerated here would destroy the idea of the internal market. It would perhaps not be an incentive for an -(e)xit of other Member States, but perhaps an incentive to plead for singular exceptions. Member States exporting workforce would prefer a protectionist regime for goods from countries with a large surplus in production. Member States with a high level of workers' income might search for exceptions for the free movement of persons. As long as the internal market as such is concerned, there is few if any leeway for exceptions at its basis. Therefore, it is logical in terms of EU law that the EU institutions, once the UK declared to leave the customs union, were very reluctant to generate any hope that the agreement for the future relationship, which shall now be negotiated would exceed the content of an ordinary free trade agreement. This is particularly important for any wish of the City of London to preserve its access to the EU's services markets.

Another point should be clear also for the EU minus UK. The free movement of persons in the internal market will hitherto have a more consequential move towards movement for economic purposes. At least, following the recent case law of the ECJ, the epoch of free movement to acquire social benefits in other Member States is probably over, and rightly so. The Court

---

13   *BDI*, Unternehmensfinanzierung, Versicherungen, Kapitalmärkte. Herausforderungen durch den Brexit, 1 February 2018, available at: https://bdi.eu/media/publikationen/?publicationtype=Positionen.

14   On this provision *Ruffert*, in: Calliess/id. (eds.), EUV/AEUV, 5th ed. 2016, Art. 3 EUV, para 22 with further references.

and the Advocates General use the expression "'benefit tourism'",[15] and I would hesitate to designate the phenomenon by this term, even not in inverted commas, for the hardship that is often behind this form of migration. But as long as there is Member States' funding of the relevant social benefits and as long as differences of wealth are that big between the Member States, intra-European migration having the only aim to acquire benefits elsewhere does not forward European integration, but may cause distortions in the overall picture. This is without prejudice of the use of the various EU funds to provide for a better life in those countries that are still poorer.

C. The Loss of Completeness and the Future of the EU

I. The Loss of Completeness

Brexit is a loss for Europe because of the particular contribution of the United Kingdom to the EU. Let us now turn to the second, even greater loss for the EU: the loss of completeness. After Brexit, the idea of a common European political order is out of reach.

It may be argued, that this was never a realistic perspective, given that not all European States are Member States of the European Union – and this would certainly not hint at countries in a difficult situation of transition such as Serbia, Montenegro or Macedonia, or even Moldova or the Ukraine, places beyond democratic rule such as Byelorussia (the Turkish question set aside) or the superpower Russia that covers a significant part of the continent. What about Iceland, Norway and Switzerland? Should the EU have developed some sort of intra-European imperialism?

The Norwegian people (5.3 million inhabitants) voted twice against joining the EU, but the country is part of the European Economic Area (EEA), as is Iceland (350,000 inhabitants) which withdrew its application for joining the EU in 2015 after eleven out of 38 chapters of negotiation had been successfully closed.[16] Switzerland (8.4 million inhabitants) even had a negative referendum on joining the EEA.[17] But Norway as Switzerland has to adhere to core rules of the internal market, either in the EEA or by bilateral agreement. Both countries are in a particular situation; Swiss neutrality is unique

---

15   *AG Ruiz-Jarabo Colomer*, Opinion to ECJ, *Collins,* Case C-138/02, [2004] ECR I-2733, para 75.

16   https://ec.europa.eu/neighbourhood-enlargement/countries/detailed-country-information/iceland_en.

17   *Oesch*, Europarecht, Vol. I, 2015, para 73.

in Europe and part of its political arrangement, and Norway is in a, though long-running, economic boom due to its wealth in crude oil and gas that is more than exceptional in its history – we do not know what happens once this is over. But the UK is different from both (or all three, with Iceland), in size and economic weight, in legal-cultural influence – and in being part of the Community and Union for more than 40 years.

So again, what is really lost with Brexit is the prospect of achieving a political and administrative space all over Europe. We know that the British government ignored what that meant for the UK; the White Paper issued several months after the referendum was literally white.[18] But what is at stake here is if the EU knows what that means for itself – and how it should react.

To my mind, it should react in a way to keep the idea of a common political and administrative area in all Europe alive, Brexit notwithstanding. True, the EU institutions and the Member States governments committed many mistakes, and the decision-making process in the refugee crisis of 2015 is far from being convincing or even attractive. But the irresponsible decision was made independent of this for completely different reasons, *viz.* the strife for power within the British Conservative Party, and it was made in the UK alone *although* the British government had negotiated concessions that went so far as to probably be in conflict with the Treaties.

In a positive sense, keeping the idea of a common political area in all Europe alive means first of all a careful reconsideration of a passage in Article 1 section 2 TEU that played a certain role in the pre-Brexit negotiations: "…the process of creating an ever closer union among the peoples of Europe,…"[19] I would submit that it is a misunderstanding to read this as the aim of reaching ever higher level of institutionalised union, a misunderstanding from both sides, from those who fear "losing control" and from those dreaming the 'Eurocrats' dream' the end of which was the title of a recent academic publication.[20] It means that an ever closer union among the peoples of Europe can

---

18 *British Prime Minister Theresa May*, The United Kingdom's exit from, and new partnership with, the European Union, 2 February 2017, Cm 9417.

19 Decision of the *Heads of State or Government*, Meeting Within the European Council, Concerning a New Settlement for the United Kingdom Within the European Union, Annex I to the Conclusions of the European Council of 18 and 19 February 2016, Doc. EUCO 1/16.

20 *Chalmers/Jachtenfuchs/Joerges* (eds.), The End of the Eurocrats' Dream, 2016.

imply a differentiated picture of political rule. This includes taking subsidiarity seriously 25 years after the principle entered the Treaty.[21] It includes modesty in formulating budgetary aims – being aware that there is not enough political power for legitimising a major increase of the budget. There is no need to fight the 'transfer union' if this is understood. All in all, it means to realise that the motto of the EU is still 'United in diversity', although the relevant article in the Constitutional treaty of 2004 never entered into force.[22]

II.   An Ambivalent Response

The response of the EU, though, is ambivalent. The Member States were rallying in the Bratislava process to bring forward concrete projects in topical policy fields such as migration and security.[23] Other activities appear to be less beneficial to the political target described. I will address the peculiarities of the EU-White Paper process in a minute. When it came to one of the first consequences of Brexit, the redistribution of seats in the European Parliament, what was decided can only be deplored. Instead of taking the unique chance of renewing the electoral system for the European Parliament, the Parliament itself and the European Council did not decide to establish constituencies all over Europe or to remedy the disequilibrium in representation.[24] Although the latter aim was pursued in redistributing 27 of the 73 British seats "to redress under-representation following demographic changes."[25], great imbalances will remain: It is not transparent at all why, for example France will get five more MEPs and Ireland two, while the Irish

---

21   Consider now: *Report of the Task Force on Subsidiarity, Proportionality and 'Doing Less More Efficiently'*, Active Subsidiarity: A new way of working, 1 August 2018, available at: https://ec.europa.eu/commission/sites/beta-political/files/report-task-force-subsidiarity-proportionality-and-doing-less-more-efficiently_en.pdf.

22   https://europa.eu/european-union/about-eu/symbols/motto_en.

23   Bratislava Declaration and Roadmap, 16 September 2016, available at: http://www.consilium.europa.eu/media/21232/160916-bratislava-declaration-and-roadmap-de.pdf.

24   With the *European Council* Decision establishing the composition of the European Parliament of 19 June 2018, Doc. EUCO 7/1/18 REV 1, all previous proposals to find creative solutions were obsolete.

25   Quoted from the *European Parliament* press release, EU elections: how many MEPs will each country get in 2019?, 1 February 2019, available at: http://www.europarl.europa.eu/news/en/headlines/eu-affairs/20180126STO94114/eu-elections-how-many-meps-will-each-country-get-in-2019.

population grew by 12 % and the French by 5.6 % only in the last ten years. Further, the limit of 96 seats in Article 14 Section 2, first subsection, fourth sentence TEU is adhered to. The German seats have to remain unchanged; there can be no doubt about that. This however, perpetuates the unequal representation in the European Parliament compared to smaller countries. Of course, this is compensated by the voting procedure in the Council, which is dependent upon the size of the population in the relevant Member State, but a great occasion was missed which is even worse as the Parliament itself is called upon to take the initiative in this field (Article 14, 2nd section, 2nd subsection TEU; Article 223 TFEU). To conclude this point: It is time to overcome problems, not to circumvent them.

III.   Consequences for EU Law Scholarship

These are more or less political questions. What does it mean for us, legal scholars? It is above all a quest for more phantasy in developing theoretical ideas on how the European Union should look like. "Unity" more than often appears to signify "like a State". This is more than comprehensible, as the nation State has such a long history and such a pertinent existence. But if we continue adhering to this, we will get lost as the Commission did in early 2017 when, instead of making a concrete proposal, it brought forward a series of scenarios as a matter of choice and discussion. In *Juncker's* State-of-the-Union address of September 2017, all options were wrapped up and a political choice of the Commission was formulated.[26] The scenario process is extremely fascinating, and also intellectually challenging, to learn how scenario x, y and z out of the five were combined to a new, sixth scenario that underlies the Commission's actual policy. We would wish that political decision-making was that far rationalised and transparent in, say, the German coalition negotiations. However, I doubt whether the different scenarios are known to more than 5 % of the general population and whether among us, scholars of EU law and other related subjects, a significant number of colleagues could tell what it was all about. Briefly, I doubt whether they played any role at all outside the Commission – certainly not in the two most important elections of 2017, in France and in Germany.

---

26   The White Paper and the Reflection papers are available at: https://ec.eu-ropa.eu/commission/white-paper-future-europe-reflections-and-scenarios-eu27_de, last accessed 7 February 2019. The speech of 13 September 2017 is available at: http://europa.eu/rapid/press-release_SPEECH-17-3165_en.htm.

The real challenge for European legal scholarship lies in further developing the theoretical and doctrinal underpinnings of the very particular construction which is the European Union. It has a constitution, but it is not a State – so what are the cornerstones of its constitutional order? How can constitutional rules and principles be conserved without what a state has, and following *Georg Jellinek's* theory of the three elements, especially without a people? How can the legislative and administrative system in such a constitutional order be built in a way that they are viable and not unclear and confusing, to the extent that justice, meaning above all equality of what is equal, and therefore normative consistency, is damaged. The European Union is not a State, not even a federal State, there is no political force that strives for creating the United States of Europe (*Martin Schulz'* statement in agony is probably not to be taken seriously), and we should stop conceiving the political construction of the Union if it were a State. But it is a constitutional and legal entity, not just a platform for Member States' negotiations at several levels. It has constitutionally based institutions, not just fora where Member States' officials come together for intergovernmental arrangements. It issues legal acts, not just contractually negotiated instruments. And there are theoretical and doctrinal links to elaborate on the non-State characteristics as on the unity-within-diversity issue: dual legitimation (see Article 10, section 2 TEU) and enhanced co-operation (Article 20 TEU).

D.   Outlook

To conclude: How will the EU develop without the United Kingdom? As lawyers, legal scholars are trained above all to make valued judgments about past events. From this, perhaps, I have the feeling as having never before given such a political paper. And unfortunately, I cannot blame my Frankfurt colleagues for the title, because we formulated it jointly. The scientifically sound answer to the initial question is that we do not know. But we can give indications following the legal-constitutional framework of the EU. It is not a measure of 'punishment' if the internal market is considered as a coherent whole. Such 'punishment' would be void of sense: There is no competing offer for successful politics in Europe the UK and other Member States could follow.[27] For this reason, I adhere to my initial assessment, that Brexit was the outcome of an irresponsible policy. The UK government refrained from

---

27   Cf. also *Pernice*, European Constitutionalism and the National Constitutions of the Member States – Implications for Brexit, in: Universidade de Coimbra, Boletin da Faculdade de Direito XCIII (2017), Vol. I, 211, 242 f.

bringing forward a critical point of view where this was necessary – because it never intended to advance EU reform.

The loss of completeness is the greatest loss of the EU, and it has to be faced with an intelligent reaction. The strongest achievements of the EU lie in the welfare effects of the internal market. New institutional arrangements are to be considered with care. Windows of opportunity for reform have to be grasped and not given away; be it the occasion for a major re-arrangement of the electoral system of the European Parliament – a chance that is almost gone –, be it a propitious political constellation – note that *Macron's* term of office is already consumed by one fifth, and we do not know who will follow. If politics develop along the lines of EU constitutional law, I am not pessimistic, but if they do not, all the more.

The impact of Brexit on British law and democracy: four effects

Mark Dawson

A.   Introduction

From the perspective of the United Kingdom, Brexit has been an event of huge proportions and significance. What for Germany and other EU countries is a matter to be managed (while hopefully limiting any collateral damage to the overall architecture of the EU) is for Britain of vast, even existential, constitutional relevance.

In the UK, for a whole generation, Brexit will be a defining political event. It is the thing by which political identity is defined. It is the substance of everyday news and everyday political conversation. It is also never-ending – by the time of Britain's actual exit in March 2019 (if it indeed occurs on that date), the population will have had 3 years of un-ending Brexit controversy.

As such, it is exceedingly difficult to measure the effect of Brexit on UK law and democracy. Any such exercise is guess-work. If Brexit is an event likely to trickle down into each and every aspect of British law, estimating the effect of Brexit is to do no less than to speculate on the very future of the UK. The numerous twists and turns the Brexit process has taken since the triggering of Article 50 in March 2017 presents a stark lesson in how complicated international negotiations can be (and the un-intended side effects they may produce).

With this having been said, this paper will attempt to briefly articulate four possible effects of Brexit on the constitutional architecture of the UK (namely B.I. the political cleavages it has produced; B.II. its effect on representative democracy; B.III. its effect on public trust and B.IV. its effect on the wider liberal constitutional order). These possible effects are grounded on the experience of Brexit to date; particularly the impact of what might loosely be termed 'the Brexit process' on UK politics and UK institutions during the phase from the June 2016 referendum to today (at the time of writing, the mid-way point of the two-year Article 50 period). The four effects add-up to a more general claim, explored in the paper's conclusion: Brexit is not only of political and economic relevance, but carries the potential to roll-back some of the more pluralist and liberal tendencies of UK public law.

B. *The four effects*

I. Effect 1 – the new political cleavage

The first effect of Brexit on British law and democracy relates precisely from its political salience, as discussed above. Brexit is such a huge topic - and such a complex and durable one - that it has begun to define how the British people see law and politics.[1] What was once a country of Labour and Tories is increasingly a country of Leavers and Remainers. This has happened in spite of two major parties who have tried to avoid these labels: Labour who have repeatedly refused to cast themselves as a party of remain (in spite of all evidence that a large majority of their voters regret the 2016 referendum) and a Conservative leader who, immediately upon taking office, has sought to be seen as part hard-Brexiteer; part pragmatist, steering negotiations in the wider national interest. We have a new cleavage in politics and it seems it will be here to stay.

This cleavage is an inevitable consequence of the referendum process. This might have been a lesson learnt by the then Prime Minister, David Cameron, who twice sought to settle divisive internal political problems through referenda: once in 2016 and again in 2014, having agreed to a referendum on Scottish independence. There too, what had once been a country divided on everyday political issues became a country divided on one issue: should Scotland remain part of the Union or become independent?

Inevitably, the process of establishing and fighting a referendum campaign polarises: it takes shades of political opinion and reduces them to one issue – where do you stand on X, are you for it or against? Inevitably, the divisions transcend the referendum itself. Once the referendum is determined (either way), a new battle begins. How is the referendum result to be interpreted and how can it be implemented faithfully? Inevitably, both sides will have different views on this question.

As a consequence, the EU referendum campaign did not resolve the question of the UK's place in Europe, but simply focused public attention on it, dividing the country into two camps. There is little indication that voters on

---

1   On the impacts of the referendum on political and national identity in the UK, see *Hobolt*, The Brexit Vote: A Divided Nation; A Divided Continent, Journal of European Public Policy Vol. 23 No. 9 (2016), 1259; *Ashcroft and Bevir*, Pluralism, National Identity and Citizenship: Britain after Brexit, The Political Quarterly Vol. 87 No. 3 (2016), 355.

either side have swayed much since the referendum result: remainers continue to think Britain should remain in the EU and leavers continue to favour
the exit door.[2] New developments – either the perilous negotiation process
or the relatively stable economic performance of the UK since the result –
have swayed neither party. In the new social media world, developments
have been happily filtered to support the pre-conceived notions of each side.

In this sense, Brexit provides lessons not just for UK politicians but for
wider comparison.[3] Referendum processes carries a dangerous capacity to
divide political opinion without providing the resources to heal and unify the
population afterwards.

II.   Effect 2 – from representative democracy to 'the will of the people'

These new cleavages though are much deeper. They also seep into UK constitutional culture. The UK has long carried one central rule in public law.
The UK, in spite of its lack of a written Constitution, has many different rules
of public law but one that is more important than the others – that Parliament
is sovereign.[4] Nothing sits above the will of Parliament as the central organ
of the UK's long tradition of representative democracy.

This is not just a rule but a way of understanding UK history. We all know
that the US believes in its exceptionalism but few realise that the UK does so
too. One of these ideas of UK exceptionalism is that it is somehow immune
from the kind of ideological extremism that befell other countries in the 20th
Century. Parliamentary sovereignty is one emblem of that – both of the cen-
trality of democracy to British life and to a *culture* of representative democracy that is seen as un-ending.

Representative democracy, as Edmurd Burke told us, implies a particular
notion of the duties of parliamentary representatives. As Burke put it in his
famous speech in 1774 to the electors of Bristol:

---

2   See e.g. the conclusions of *Menon and Wager*, Brexit and British politics, in:
     Menon (ed.), Brexit and UK Public Opinion, 2018, p. 8.
3   See other work on the link between referendum processes and political polariza-
     tion e.g. *Atikcan and Oge*, Referendum Campaigns in Polarized Societies: The
     Case of Turkey, Turkish Studies Vol. 13 No.3 (2012); *Lemennicier*, Political Po-
     larization and the French Rejection of the European Constitution, European Jour-
     nal of Political Economy Vol. 21 No. 4, (2005).
4   On the pre-eminence of this rule, see *Dicey*, Introduction to the Law of the Con-
     stitution2013, pp. 27-50.

"Certainly, gentlemen, it ought to be the happiness and glory of a representative to live in the strictest union, the closest correspondence, and the most unreserved communication with his constituents. Their wishes ought to have great weight with him; their opinion, high respect; their business, unremitted attention. It is his duty to sacrifice his repose, his pleasures, his satisfactions, to theirs; and above all, ever, and in all cases, to prefer their interest to his own. But his unbiassed opinion, his mature judgment, his enlightened conscience, he ought not to sacrifice to you, to any man, or to any set of men living. These he does not derive from your pleasure; no, nor from the law and the constitution. They are a trust from Providence, for the abuse of which he is deeply answerable. Your representative owes you, not his industry only, but his judgment; and he betrays, instead of serving you, if he sacrifices it to your opinion."[5]

In a representative democracy of this kind, representatives are certainly accountable to their voters but first and foremost they are accountable to their own conscious and their own judgment as to what the good of the nation requires.

Brexit has also challenged this element of the UK's democratic tradition. This is so in the sense that the referendum process has brought another competing idea of democracy into British political life (an idea that previous generations may have considered French and therefore antithetical to all things British): the idea of the will of the people.

It is interesting that the most seemingly British of institutions – newspapers like the Daily Mail – are the ones most protective of the idea that sovereignty in the UK no longer flows from Parliament; it flows directly from the people.[6] Whenever Brexit has been challenged – as it was when Gina Miller brought her case before the Supreme Court or it is at the time of writing by amendments seeking to keep the UK in the Customs Union – this idea of the will of the British people is brought forward.

Those against Brexit – even if they have a parliamentary majority – are trying to subvert the democratic will. They are trying to overturn the settled result of the referendum (in the words of that same newspaper, the Daily Mail, opponents of Brexit are not just opponents but 'saboteurs').[7] Here, a very different idea of democracy is being invoked – representatives do their democratic duty not when they do what they think is 'right' by their conscience but rather when they follow the preferences of their constituents.

---

5   *Burke*, Speech to the Electors of Bristol, available at: http://press-pubs.uchicago.edu/founders/documents/v1ch13s7.html, last accessed 8 February 2019, like all online material cited in this contribution.
6   See e.g. *Daily Mail*, Ignore the Will of the People at your Peril,12 June2018; *The Sun*, Great Britain or Great Betrayal, 12 June2018.
7   *Daily Mail*, Crush the Saboteurs,19 April 2017.

This majoritarian idea of democracy is also one of the genies of Brexit that will be difficult to put back in the bottle. The idea of British democracy as something mediated through representatives is increasingly having to fight with an idea that has quite populist overtones – it is the job of politicians to do the bidding of the majority plus one (with any deviation potentially trea-sonous).

Once again of course, this could be seen as an effect of the politics of ref-erenda. It is not only that referenda reduce different opinions to a simple bi-nary: they also provide a unique legitimacy to a weight of opinion (in the Brexit case, 52% of the population) that in many systems would by no means be seen as sufficient a consensus to allow for major constitutional change.[8] The referendum allowed the slow process of deliberation and exchange that would normally typify constitutional amendment to be by-passed in a dra-matic fashion.

III.   Effect 3 – Trust in Politics

Trust in politics in the UK is notoriously low.[9] While plenty of European states carry populations with a healthy scepticism about their politicians, there remains a depth of cynicism about politics in the UK that surpasses its neighbours. This has been fostered by a number of factors, from the Thatch-erite drive to divest the state of public functions from the 1980s to the parlia-mentary expenses scandal that hit the Westminster Parliament in the 2010s. A common phrase heard on UK streets is that 'they are all as bad as each other'. On television, politicians are frequently interviewed as if every word could be a lie.[10] There is a toxic lack of faith in political integrity.

Brexit carries the potential to make this lack of faith even worse than it already is. The main reason is that Brexit was based on an undeliverable promise: the promise that by leaving the EU, the UK can 'take back control'.

---

8   See e.g. the inclusion of French EU membership within the text of the French Constitution (thus requiring constitutional modification for any future French withdrawal).

9   See *Institute of Government*, Public Trust in Public Servants, available at: https://www.instituteforgovernment.org.uk/blog/public-trust-public-servants-%E2%80%93-six-graphs.

10   See e.g. the conclusions statement of *Jeremy Paxman* (one of the UK's leading journalists) available at: http://blogs.bl.uk/thenewsroom/2014/07/why-is-this-ly-ing-bastard-lying-to-me.html.

Control was the leitmotif of the leave campaign and has been repeated ever since as the essence of the result.[11]

Yet, what is control? It has been defined to mean that any sovereignty loss; any binding of UK politics by an external force; is intolerable.[12] This is the box that has bound the UK government during the Brexit negotiations. The UK requires a degree of regulatory alignment with the rest of EU to avoid a hard border with Ireland but this would conflict with the sovereignty gains Brexit was promised to provide. The UK economy needs a comprehensive customs arrangement but this would conflict with the freedom of the UK to make its own trade deals with other countries (including the larger economies of the former Commonwealth). Any type of useful trading arrangement will involve sovereignty loss yet any such loss is by definition anti-thetical to the original goal of Brexit, as conceived by its architects.

Brexit promised democracy. If it carries a universal, non-nativist goal, it is rooted in a promise of self-determination. Yet any of the feasible options that now lay on the table in terms of the UK's future relationship with its European partners would involve shifting the UK, to a greater or lesser degree, from a rule-maker (albeit one sometimes out-voted in the Council) to a rule-taker; a state that has to submit to rules made elsewhere without having a say in making them.

This is inevitably a recipe for deepening suspicion of politicians. It links with a point Wolfgang Streeck has often made regarding the loss of faith in democracy in the developed world. Increasing disenchantment with the democratic process is linked not just to an increasing distance between politicians and voters but to the state's lost steering capacity: politicians just cannot deliver (and don't have the tools to deliver) what they say they can deliver.[13]

Brexit is the ultimate manifestation of this conundrum. Ironically, it breeds exactly the feelings that it is designed to remedy: namely the notion that, in the face of economic globalization, democratic control of the basic conditions of human life is increasingly impossible. The feelings of helplessness that Brexit sought to answer yet continues to foster seems a likely driver of further disenchantment with politics and politicians in the years to come.

---

11   See e.g. the very name of the main website of the leave campaign: www.voteleavetakecontrol.org/.

12   See Daily Express, Rees Mogg demands end concessions to EU: Freedom from Brussels or be a Vassal State, 19. March 2018.

13   On this thesis, see *Streeck*, The Crisis of Democratic Capitalism, New Left Review 71 (2011), 5.

IV.   Effect 4 – Checks and Balances

The final effect of Brexit on UK law and democracy worth commenting upon is related to this and particularly to the impact of the Brexit process on UK law. One of the themes of contemporary comparative scholarship on constitutional law in Europe concerns the confrontation between constitutional frameworks and the rise of populist movements and parties.[14] This research field is of obvious relevance to Central and Eastern Europe but also to established democracies. What would happen for example if an Orban or similar illiberal populist came to power in a state such as Germany? How easily could he overturn the constitutional order and start appointing friendly judges or eroding other independent institutions? As Max Steinbeis has observed in a recent commentary, there is nothing dictator proof about established democracies, such as Germany – even with the protection of an extensive German constitutional order, the erosion of democratic norms may be easier than you think.[15]

It is worth extending this hypothetical exercise to the UK. If Orbanization is possible in Germany, it seems positively easy in the UK. In the UK, we have a country that has no written Constitution, and that has a much weaker form of judicial review, especially when it comes to parliamentary acts. The UK has no formal federal structure, in the sense that the devolved administrations enjoy their powers at the behest of a normal Westminster Parliamentary Act (which could simply be removed from the statute books).

Furthermore, the UK carries no formal separation of powers, and a lower house that is far stronger than its unelected upper chamber. It has no proportional electoral system, necessitating the government to find alliances and compromises with other parties (with the result that parties with as little as 36% of the vote have enjoyed comfortable parliamentary majorities). As the former Lord Chancellor, Lord Hailsham, once described it, the UK is an 'elective dictatorship'; once a government is in place, and carries a majority, there are few, if any, real constraints, on its ability to promote its chosen agenda.

The point here is not that the UK is on the brink of a likely authoritarian take-over but that one impact of Brexit is that is makes the already limited constraints on executive power in the UK even weaker. This is so because

---

14   See e.g. *von Bogdandy and Sonnevend* (eds.), Constitutional Crisis in the European Constitutional Area: Theory, Law and Politics in Hungary and Romania, 2015.

15   *Steinbeis*, It Can Happen Here, available at: https://verfassungsblog.de/it-can-happen-here/.

Brexit runs directly against a pluralist current in UK constitutionalism developing for at least two decades, or a tendency to challenge the model of the elective dictatorship Hailsham laid out in the late 70s.

There are two principal ways in which executive power has been increasingly constrained in the UK in the last few decades. One is constraint from above i.e. imposing obligations on government emerging from supra-national and international law, including human rights law. Another is constraint from below i.e. the emergence of the devolved administrations, with their own capacities to challenge the government when it strays into areas of devolved powers.

Both of these levels of control are weakened by Brexit. The clearest comes from above. EU law has been a way of UK and foreign citizens challenging UK law in general, and discriminatory UK laws in particular, ever since the UK's entry into the Communities. Many of the most famous cases in EU law, for example in the field of citizenship or in the field of free movement of persons, have been cases that started in the UK and were then referred to Luxembourg.[16] EU equality law has had a profound effect on the UK, creating a layer of rights, for parents, for workers and for minorities that can no longer be guaranteed, even if they are now converted into UK law via the great repeal bill (an attempt to align UK and existing EU law).

Even if the withdrawal bill (or certain aspects of it such as the Chapter on Citizens Rights[17]) encourages the UK Courts to consider case-law of the ECJ, there is a considerable risk of a more insular UK legal order; one that looks less and less to other jurisdictions and international courts for inspiration in interpreting and developing its law.

The possibility that EU law provided, and that the EU Charter of Fundamental Rights enshrines – of using EU law as a device to control the UK government – is one that Brexit removes. It is particularly concerning given that one of the central projects of the current UK Prime Minister in the past has been the removal of the UK from the ECHR system, which would remove another layer of checks from above. These developments challenge the use by the UK Courts of both the Charter and the ECHR to develop tools for the

---

16   See e.g. ECJ, Zhu & Chen, Case C-200/02, EU:C:2004:639; ECJ, Collins, Case C-138/02, EU:C:2004:172.

17   See Chapter 6 of the Government's White Paper, The United Kingdom's Exit from and New Partnership with the European Union, available at: https://assets.publishing.service.gov.uk/government/uploads/system/uploads/attachment_data/file/589191/The_United_Kingdoms_exit_from_and_partnership_with_the_EU_Web.pdf.

judicial review of UK parliamentary acts (many of which did not exist prior to the UK's integration into the wider European legal order).

There is also the danger, however, that Brexit challenges control from below. Consider for example, the recent Miller judgement of the UK Supreme Court.[18] One arguments brought forward in Miller was that the Sewell Convention constrained the ability of the UK government to directly trigger Art. 50 and therefore start the process of leaving the Union.[19] The Sewell Convention is the idea that the devolved administrations must be consulted by acts of the Westminster government that concerns areas of devolved powers.

In Miller, the Supreme Court agreed with the government that this was merely a constitutional convention – a practice that is habitually followed but not a strict legal obligation (and therefore one that could be enforced by the Court). This could be seen as a missed opportunity. Miller could have been a chance for the UK Courts to use Brexit as an opportunity to enhance the rights of the devolved administrations – to argue that significant substantive and constitutional changes affecting the UK as a whole required negotiation and agreement between the UK's constituent parts. Surely, there is no greater constitutional change to have occurred in the last decades than the UK's decision to leave the EU: this is a decision, however, from which the constituent nations of the UK have been largely excluded (in spite of the fact that two of those nations, Scotland and North Ireland, delivered large majorities for remain).[20]

At the very least, there remains a danger that, as powers are repatriated to the UK, there remain significant disagreements between devolved administrations and the UK government over how those powers are exercised. This concerns in particular the so-called 'Henry VIII' clauses i.e. areas where EU legislation converted into UK law via the great repeal bill can be amended directly by ministers, without the approval of Parliament. Just as MPs have complained that such powers frustrate the scrutiny powers of Parliament so they carry the capacity to ignite tensions over who has the power to make such amendments: Westminster, or Belfast, Cardiff and Edinburgh?

---

18   This argument is developed in more depth in *Dawson*, Brexit in the Supreme Court: An Opportunity Missed?, available at: https://verfassungsblog.de/brexit-in-the-supreme-court-an-opportunity-missed/.

19   *R (Miller) v Secretary of State* [2017] UKSC 5 at [10].

20   See e.g. the conclusions of the UK's Parliaments EU Select Committee, Brexit: Devolution, available at: https://publications.parliament.uk/pa/ld201719/ldselect/ldeucom/9/9.pdf.

Brexit carries a rhetoric of taking back control (and of restoring 'local' forms of democracy) but most of that control is being handed to the Westminster government; a government that lacks the checks and balances of other European governments or a system of proportional representation to limit the power of one political group. There is a risk that the more pluralistic legal and political order the UK has built in the last decades will be eroded.

C.   Conclusion

As indicated in this paper's introduction, there is a certain folly in predicting how Brexit will affect UK law and democracy. Such a gargantuan exercise of economic and legal upheaval is likely to have numerous unknown consequences and side-effects. Just as Brexit has split the UK population into two divided campaigns, so the historical evaluation of Brexit's effects are likely to be split, with 'remainers' pinning every difficulty the UK faces on its EU exit, and 'leavers' painting any success as a vindication of their experiment in constitutional change.

If one must, however, hazard guesses, this contribution's guess is that Brexit will make the UK a less democratic, less constrained and less liberal state. If successful democracies are ones where the government faces an obligation to listen to other voices, including those of national outsiders, Brexit makes this listening exercise less likely. And if successful democracies create mechanisms to disperse as well as concentrate power, Brexit undermines this aspect of the UK's emerging constitutional culture (another separation from the European mainstream). For those who care about UK law and democracy, and its future, one can simply hope that this prediction is wrong. The long and winding road of Brexit has many turns (and many surprises) yet to come.

Brexit and Devolution

*Gordon Anthony**

A.   *Introduction*

The title of this essay collection – *"Brexit, and What it Means"* – is a play on words ("Brexit means Brexit") that provides a bridging point to the very real complexities of UK withdrawal from the EU. Within the UK itself, one of the areas of greatest difficulty has been intergovernmental relations, as "devolution" in Northern Ireland, Scotland and Wales coincided with different "national" votes in the EU referendum of 23 June 2016 (England and Wales both voting "leave"; Northern Ireland and Scotland voting "remain").[1] Politically, this led to calls for *referenda* on Scottish independence and Irish unification,[2] although those were to be overtaken by more immediate debates about how to give legal effect to withdrawal. In the first instance, there was a question about what role, if any, the devolved legislatures should play in the context of giving notification under Article 50 TEU, where the Supreme Court in *Miller* ruled that this was pre-eminently a matter of politics rather than law.[3] Moreover, once notification had been given, a question arose about whether the mode of repatriating powers from the EU was something upon which the devolved institutions could legislate, or whether the Westminster

---

*   I would wish to thank Professor Dr Stefan Kadelbach for his kind invitation to speak at the XVII Walter Hallstein-Kolloquium at the Goethe Universität, 15-16 March 2018. My thanks are also due to the participants at the colloquium, who posed a number of interesting and insightful questions that I have tried to address in this chapter. Any errors are mine.

1   For the results see: http://www.bbc.co.uk/news/politics/eu_referendum/results (last accessed 16 January 2019, like all online material cited in this contribution).

2   See The Guardian, Nicola Sturgeon says she would consider 2017 Scottish referendum, 17 July 2016, available at https://www.theguardian.com/politics/2016/jul/17/nicola-sturgeon-would-consider-2017-scottish-independence-referendum-brexit; and, BBC News, McGuinness: Case for border poll strengthened, 24 June 2016, available at http://www.bbc.co.uk/news/uk-politics-eu-referendum-36615515.

3   *R (Miller) v Secretary of State*; *In re McCord*; *In re Agnew* [2017] UKSC 5, [2018] AC 61.

Parliament was exclusively competent to do so. That question was to be answered in a further ruling of the Supreme Court, which held that, while the Scottish Parliament was competent to legislate in relation to returning EU law, its powers were greatly constrained by the model of sovereignty that underpins the Scotland Act 1998.[4] A further question – addressed but not (yet?) resolved by the controversial Withdrawal Agreement of November 2018 – has concerned the vexed issue of the Irish border: can EU withdrawal be achieved in a manner that is consistent with the Belfast/Good Friday Agreement 1998, or can withdrawal only unsettle that constitutional accord?

The purpose of this chapter is to explain in more detail the background to these questions and to outline the answers that have so far been given. In doing so, it provides some insight into the nature of the UK constitution and how Brexit is returning that constitution to an orthodoxy that complicates the devolution settlement.[5] Prior to the EU referendum, devolution had developed in such a way that it had been compared to a nascent form of federalism and had attracted judicial references to a "divided sovereignty" within the UK.[6] While the case law of the courts had not gone so far as formally to depart from from the Diceyan doctrine of Parliamentary sovereignty – *viz.*, the well-known idea that the Westminster Parliament can make or unmake any law whatsoever[7] – it had indicated that the devolved institutions had a democratic mandate that corresponded with (sub?) nationally defined political preferences.[8] However, with Brexit leading to a judicial emphasis on the sovereign legal power of the Westminster Parliament, this has undermined those emerging and countervailing narratives about the nature of devolution. The implications have perhaps been most pronounced in the Northern Irish

---

4   *The UK Withdrawal from the European Union (Legal Continuity) (Scotland) Bill – A Reference by the Attorney General and the Advocate General for Scotland* [2018] UKSC 64 [2019] 2 WLR 1.

5   For further analysis see *Anthony*, Sovereignty, Consent, and Constitutions: The Northern Ireland References, in Elliott, Williams and Young (eds.), The UK Constitution after Miller: Brexit and Beyond, 2018, p. 181 and *Anthony*, Brexit and the Common Law Constitution, European Public Law 24 (2018), 673.

6   For "divided sovereignty" see *Jackson v Attorney-General* [2005] UKHL 56, [2006] 1 AC 262, 302, para 102, *Lord Steyn*. For extra-judicial mention of federalism see *Lady Hale*, The UK Supreme Court in the UK Constitution, 12 October 2012, p. 23, at https://www.supremecourt.uk/docs/speech-121012.pdf.

7   *Dicey*, Introduction to the Study of the Law of the Constitution, 10th ed, 1959.

8   See *Axa General Insurance v HM Advocate* [2011] UKSC 46, [2012] 1 AC 868, 911, para 46, *Lord Hope* and [2012] 1 AC 868, 944, para 146, *Lord Reed*. See also *Re Recovery of Medical Costs for Asbestos Diseases (Wales) Bill* [2015] UKSC 3, [2015] AC 1016, 1059-1060, paras 118-120, *Lord Thomas*.

context, where ideas of fluid sovereignty defined the Belfast/Good Friday Agreement which had taken EU membership as an assumed – and ongoing – reality.[9]

The chapter is structured as follows. The first section provides an outline of pre-Brexit debates about sovereignty and devolution, where it relates the significance of judicial comments about "divided sovereignty" to what is known as the "Sewel convention". As will be seen, that convention governs the circumstances under which the Westminster Parliament can legislate for devolved matters, and it was central to the *Miller* case and the Supreme Court's emphasis on the distinction between law and politics. However, this is where the return to Diceyan sovereignty was at its most apparent, and the second section of the chapter examines the *Miller* case in some detail by way of drawing comparisons with the earlier authorities on sovereignty. The third section then considers the subsequent debate about which legislature(s) were competent to legislate for the domestic legal effects of withdrawal from the EU, where it notes how the Supreme Court's more recent ruling on that question marked a further departure from any nuanced conception of sovereignty. The last substantive section reflects upon the particular challenges that Brexit presents in the context of Northern Ireland, while the conclusion offers some final observations about Brexit, devolution, and the contemporary UK constitution.

B.   Devolution Pre-Brexit

The first point that might be made about devolution is that it has often described as "a process, not an event".[10] This phrase reflects the fact that devolution has evolved greatly since its introduction in 1998, as varying political pressures in Northern Ireland, Scotland and Wales have resulted in changes to each of the (asymmetrical) schemes for devolution.[11] The most prominent

---

9   For this and related themes see *Harvey* (ed.), Human Rights, Equality and Democratic Renewal in Northern Ireland, 2001.

10   For use of the phrase see, eg, House of Commons Briefing Paper No 08318, 11 July 2018, "A process, not an event": Devolution in Wales, 1998-2018, available at https://researchbriefings.parliament.uk/ResearchBriefing/Summary/CBP-8318 #fullreport.

11   The most important legislation for each jurisdiction is, respectively, the Northern Ireland Act 1998 (as amended), the Scotland Act 1998 (as amended), and the Gov-

changes have all been designed to increase and consolidate power at the devolved levels, where the Scottish independence referendum of 2014 provided
an impetus for so-called "devo-max" in Scotland but also had implications
for devolution more generally. At their height, such changes have sought to
create space for national (and nationalistic) preferences,[12] although they have
all occurred within a constitutional framework that reasserts the final law-
making power of the Westminster Parliament.[13] It is thus here that the tension
around Brexit has had many of its origins: while devolution is about empow-
ering local institutions and their nationally defined electorates, it remains tied
to a centralised model of sovereignty that renders it different in form from
federalism.[14]

The case law that had earlier suggested that devolution might require a
revised approach to sovereignty had taken its lead (perhaps now paradoxi-
cally) from the constitutional implications of EU membership.[15] This, famously, is the realm of *Lord Steyn's* opinion in *Jackson*, where his Lordship
observed that the Westminster Parliament's powers had been limited by the
demands of EU law and that, "The settlement contained in the Scotland Act
1998 also points to a divided sovereignty [within the UK] [...]. The classic
account [...] of the doctrine of the supremacy of Parliament, pure and absolute
as it was, can now be seen to be out of place in the modern [UK]".[16] In historical terms, *Lord Steyn's* comments were at one with the pronouncements

---

ernment of Wales Act 2006 (as amended). Note that Northern Ireland had previous experience with devolution from the date of its creation in 1921: see *Hadfield*,
The Constitution of Northern Ireland, 1989.

12   *Tierney*, Devolution in historical and political context, in: Elliott and Thomas,
Public Law, 3rd ed, 2017, p. 332.

13   Northern Ireland Act 1998, s 5(6); Scotland Act 1998, s 28(7); Government of
Wales Act 2006, s 107(5).

14   For the differences between the two see *Hadfield*, The Foundations of Review,
Devolved Power and Delegated Power, in: Forsyth (ed.), Judicial Review and the
Constitution, 2000, pp. 193, 194. See also *The UK Withdrawal from the European
Union (Legal Continuity) (Scotland) Bill – A Reference by the Attorney General
and the Advocate General for Scotland* [2018] UKSC 64, (note 4) para 41.

15   On which see, most prominently, *R v Secretary of State for Transport, ex p Fac-
tortame (No 2)* [1991] 1 AC 603; *Thoburn v Sunderland CC* [2003] QB 151; *R
(Buckinghamshire CC) v Secretary of State for Transport* [2014] UKSC 3, [2014]
1 WLR 324; and *Pham v Secretary of State for Home Department* [2015] UKSC
19, [2015] 1 WLR 1591. For commentary see *Craig*, Britain in the European Union, in: Jowell, Oliver and O'Cinneide (eds.), The Changing Constitution, *8th* ed.,
2015, ch 4.

16   *Jackson v Attorney-General* [2005] UKHL 56, [2006] 1 AC 262, 302, para 102.

of some Scottish judges[17], and they resonated with a number of contemporary statements about the devolution legislation for Northern Ireland, Scotland and Wales. For instance, in *Thoburn*, *Laws LJ* identified the Scotland Act 1998 and [what is now] the Government of Wales Act 2006 as "constitutional statutes" that are not subject to some of the ordinary rules of statutory interpretation[18]; while, in *Robinson*, *Lord Bingham* described the Northern Ireland Act 1998 as a "constitution" that should be interpreted "generously and purposively, bearing in mind the values which the constitutional provisions are intended to embody".[19] Moreover, in *Axa*, the Supreme Court considered the question of how closely the courts should scrutinise the choices of the devolved legislatures, and ruled that judicial restraint would often be merited.[20] The challenge here was to an Act of the Scottish Parliament that allowed individuals to sue for harms suffered whilst working in Scotland's heavy industries, but, in dismissing the challenge, the Supreme Court drew attention to the Scottish Parliament's democratic legitimacy and mandate.[21] The Court here said that, whilst the Scottish Parliament is not legally sovereign, it is a "self-standing democratically elected legislature"[22] and that, "(w)ithin the limits set by the [Scotland Act] ... its power to legislate is as ample as it could possibly be".[23]

The closest the pre-Brexit case law came to developing *Lord Steyn's* comments about divided sovereignty was in *Re Recovery of Medical Costs for Asbestos Diseases (Wales) Bill*.[24] This ruling was given when the Counsel General for Wales referred to the Supreme Court the legality of a Bill that

---

17   See, eg, *MacCormick v Lord Advocate* 1953 SC 396, 411, *Lord Cooper*: "[T]he principle of the unlimited sovereignty of Parliament is a distinctively English principle which has no counterpart in Scottish constitutional law".

18   *Thoburn v Sunderland CC* [2003] QB 151, 186. Compare Lord Hope's subsequent comments in *Imperial Tobacco Ltd v Lord Advocate* [2012] UKSC 61, 2013 SC (UKSC) 153, paras 12-15. And see also the other cases cited at n 66 below, and corresponding text.

19   *Robinson v Secretary of State for Northern Ireland* [2002] UKHL 32, [2002] NI 390, 398, para 11. See also Lord Hoffmann's comments at [2002] NI 390, 402, para 25.

20   *Axa General Insurance v HM Advocate* [2011] UKSC 46, [2012] 1 AC 868.

21   The legislation in question was the Damages (Asbestos-related Conditions) (Scotland) Act 2009.

22   *Axa General Insurance v HM Advocate* [2012] 1 AC 868, 911, para 46, *Lord Hope*.

23   *Axa General Insurance v HM Advocate* [2012] 1 AC 868, 944, para 146, *Lord Reed*.

24   *Re Recovery of Medical Costs for Asbestos Diseases (Wales) Bill* [2015] UKSC 3, [2015] AC 1016.

would have allowed the Welsh Ministers to recover from employers and insurers some of the costs of treating persons for work-related illnesses on the National Health Service. One of the questions was whether the Bill constituted a disproportionate interference with rights under Article 1 of Protocol 1 ECHR, where *Lord Mance* (for the majority) held that it did. In doing so, his Lordship accepted that he should give "weight" to the Welsh Assembly's public interest choice in passing the Bill[25], but he considered that he could form a view on its proportionality without addressing the "difficult" question whether "there is a relevant distinction between cases concerning primary legislation by the United Kingdom Parliament and other legislative and executive decisions".[26] In contrast, *Lord Thomas*, for the minority, examined this constitutional question in some detail and commented that "great weight" should be given to the public interest choice of the Welsh Assembly. Stating that he "would find it difficult to make any logical distinction in the context of the United Kingdom's devolved constitutional structure between [the devolved] legislatures and the United Kingdom Parliament in according weight to the evaluation of the different choices and interests in respect of matters which are within the primary competence of the legislatures",[27] his Lordship concluded that he could not "see why in principle the United Kingdom Parliament in making legislative choices in relation to England (in relation to matters such as the funding of the NHS in England) is to be accorded a status which commands greater weight than would be accorded to the Scottish Parliament and the Northern Ireland and Welsh Assemblies in relation respectively to Scotland, Northern Ireland and Wales".[28] On one reading, this was an approach that had started to equate devolution with a nascent federalism in the UK.[29]

Of course, such developments did not occur in isolation and had parallels in the political world, most notably in the form of the Sewel convention. As noted above, that convention governs the circumstances under which the Westminster Parliament can legislate for devolved matters, where its fundamental purpose is to ensure that devolution works in a manner that respects

---

25 *Re Recovery of Medical Costs for Asbestos Diseases (Wales) Bill* [2015] UKSC 3, [2015] AC 1016, 1046, para 67.

26 *Re Recovery of Medical Costs for Asbestos Diseases (Wales) Bill* [2015] UKSC 3, [2015] AC 1016, 1041, para 56.

27 *Re Recovery of Medical Costs for Asbestos Diseases (Wales) Bill* [2015] UKSC 3, [2015] AC 1016, 1059-1060, paras 118-119.

28 *Re Recovery of Medical Costs for Asbestos Diseases (Wales) Bill* [2015] UKSC 3, [2015] AC 1016, 1060, para 122.

29 For an extra-judicial pronouncement to like effect see *Lady Hale,* (note 6).

the roles of the UK Parliament and the devolved legislatures. The convention takes its name from a statement that was made by *Lord Sewel* during a Parliamentary debate about (what became) the Scotland Act 1998, when he said: "as happened in Northern Ireland earlier in the century, we would expect a convention to be established that Westminster would not normally legislate with regard to devolved matters in Scotland without the consent of the Scottish parliament".[30] The convention was subsequently written into a Memorandum of Understanding on intergovernmental relations in terms that make it clear that, "The United Kingdom Parliament retains authority to legislate on any issue, whether devolved or not. It is ultimately for Parliament to decide what use to make of that power". However, the Memorandum of Understanding also acknowledges that "Parliament's decision to devolve certain matters [means] that Parliament itself will in future be more restricted in its field of operation".[31] The Sewel convention thus operates most obviously when an Act of the UK Parliament will have effects in a policy area that has been devolved to one or more of the devolved legislatures, as the UK government is at that stage expected to raise the issue of consent with its devolved counterpart(s). Devolution guidance notes now also accept that the Sewel convention should operate when an Act of the UK Parliament will either expand or diminish legislative and/or executive powers at the devolved level. [32] In contrast, it is generally accepted that the Sewel convention does not operate in relation to subordinate legislation – though it has since been noted that that exception may be "strained" by Brexit, where, as will be seen below, the European Union (Withdrawal) Act 2018 envisages use of subordinate legislation to amend the statute book in areas of overlapping devolved and central government competence.[33]

It is important to be clear about just how prominent the Sewel convention was to become in the years that preceded the Brexit referendum. While it initially took the form of only soft law – and was thereby one of the so-called

---

30   *HL Debates*, vol no 592, part no 191, col 791 (21 July 1998).
31   The Memorandum of Understanding is available at https://www.gov.uk/government/publications/devolution-memorandum-of-understanding-and-supplementary-agreement.
32   See Devolution Guidance Notes 8-10, available at https://www.gov.uk/government/publications/devolution-guidance-notes.
33   See further *'The Great Repeal Bill' and Delegated Powers, House of Lords Committee on the Constitution*, 9th Report of 2016-2017, HL Paper 123, paras 115-122, available at https://publications.parliament.uk/pa/ld201617/ldselect/ldconst/123/12302.htm.

"conventions of the constitution" – it was later to be codified in the devolution legislation that applies in Scotland and Wales (but not Northern Ireland).[34] This was one out-working of the evolutionary process of devolution
that was mentioned above, which had developed at pace after the Scottish
independence referendum of 2014. One response to that referendum had been
the creation of a commission to enquire into devolved powers in Scotland
and, when it reported, it recommended that there should be statutory recognition both of the permanence of the devolved institutions in Scotland and of
the Sewel convention.[35] Those recommendations were subsequently accepted by the UK government and legislated for by the Westminster Parliament, with the result that section 28(8) of the Scotland Act 1998 now provides that "the Parliament of the United Kingdom will not normally legislate
with regard to devolved matters without the consent of the Scottish Parliament".[36] By the time of the Brexit referendum, Sewel had therefore been expressly written into parts of the legislative scheme of devolution, even if its
operation was still conditioned by the use of the word "normally".

C. *Miller and Sovereignty*

It was against this backdrop that the *Miller* case came to be argued.[37] The
central question in the case was whether the UK government could rely upon
the Royal prerogative/executive treaty-making powers to provide notification of withdrawal under Article 50 TEU, or whether it could do so only on
the basis of an Act of the Wesminster Parliament. In holding that an Act of
the Westminster Parliament was required, the Supreme Court began by con-
firming the well-established rule that prerogative powers cannot generally be
used to change statute law or the common law, or to remove rights from individuals.[38] While the government had argued that such limitations did not

---

34   On conventions of the constitution see *Leyland*, The Constitution of the United
     Kingdom: A Contextual Analysis, 3rd ed, 2016, ch 2.
35   See the report of "the Smith Commission", available at http://webarchive.nation-
     alarchives.gov.uk/20151202171029/http://www.smith-commission.scot/wp-con-
     tent/uploads/2014/11/The_Smith_Commission_Report-1.pdf.
36   On Wales see Government of Wales Act 2006, s 107(6).
37   *R (Miller) v Secretary of State; In re McCord; In re Agnew* [2017] UKSC 5, [2018]
     AC 61.
38   *R (Miller) v Secretary of State; In re McCord; In re Agnew* [2017] UKSC 5, [2018]
     AC 61, 136-143, paras 34-59.

apply because the case concerned only the narrow prerogative power to withdraw from international treaties, the Supreme Court did not consider that the exercise of the power would have those limited effects. In reaching that conclusion, the Court was influenced by the (now erroneous) assumption that, once notification is given under Article 50(2) TEU, it cannot be rescinded and must inevitably lead to withdrawal in accordance with the wider terms of Article 50 TEU.[39] For the Court, this meant that notification would have unavoidable consequences in domestic law in the sense that the Treaties would cease to apply once the timelines within Article 50(3) TEU had expired, irrespective of what Parliament may choose to do after notification. As those Treaties had effect in UK law under the terms of the European Communities Act 1972 – the legislation that discharges the obligations of membership within the domestic legal system – it followed that only the Westminster Parliament could authorise withdrawal. This was all the more so given that EU law guarantees a range of rights as, to the extent that the Court accepted that the content of such rights could change as EU law itself changes, it did not accept that they could be negated by "ministers unilaterally deciding that the United Kingdom should withdraw from the EU Treaties".[40] Nor did the Court accept the alternative argument that ministers had acquired a power of notification under the legislation that had provided for the referendum on membership (*viz.*, the European Union Referendum Act 2015). That Act was said to be silent on the legal effects of a "leave" vote and something express was required.[41]

The corresponding devolution question in the case – which arose on a reference from the courts in Northern Ireland[42] – concerned the applicability of the Sewel convention in the event that notification could be given only on the

---

39 *R (Miller) v Secretary of State*; *In re McCord*; *In re Agnew* [2017] UKSC 5, [2018] AC 61, 134 (at para 26) & 153 (at para 94). On the scope for a Member State to revoke an Article 50 notification see Case C-621/18, *Wightman v Secretary of State for Exiting the European Union* [2018] 3 WLR 1965.

40 *R (Miller) v Secretary of State*; *In re McCord*; *In re Agnew* [2017] UKSC 5, [2018] AC 61, 150, para 83.

41 *R (Miller) v Secretary of State*; *In re McCord*; *In re Agnew* [2017] UKSC 5, [2018] AC 61, 158-160, paras 116-125.

42 There were in fact two references from Northern Ireland: *Re Agnew* (reference by the High Court on the application of the Attorney General for Northern Ireland) and *Re McCord* (reference by the Court of Appeal for Northern Ireland). The two references raised five questions in total, but only that related to Sewel is of relevance here. On the other questions, and their disposal, see *McCrudden* and *Halberstam*, Miller and Northern Ireland: A Critical Constitutional Response, 8 *UK Supreme Court Yearbook* 1 (2017); and *Anthony*, (note 5).

authority of an Act of the Westminster Parliament.[43] (The essence of the question was whether the UK government was legally obliged to seek the consent of the devolved legislatures for the Westminster legislation given that EU withdrawal would have the effect of expanding devolved competences.[44]) The Supreme Court started its analysis by noting that, read on its original terms, the Sewel convention means that the UK Parliament will "not normally legislate with regard to devolved matters without the agreement of the [relevant] devolved legislature".[45] While the Court did not go into detail on whether the Sewel convention should be given a broad or more narrow reading, it did note that the Scottish Parliament and Welsh Assembly had previously passed Sewel motions in relation to Acts of the Westminster Parliament that had specifically addressed their devolved powers (albeit that they had not passed motions for Acts that had affected their powers by reason of implementing changes to the competences of EU institutions).[46] This was, however, essentially an exercise in context-setting, as the remainder of the ruling focused on the political nature of the Sewel convention and its resultant non-enforceability in law. In adopting that position, the Court acknowledged that judges could "recognise the operation of a political convention in the context of deciding a legal question" and that the Sewel convention "has an important role in facilitating harmonious relations between the UK Parliament and the devolved legislatures".[47] Nevertheless, the Court was ultimately of the view that, "Judges [...] are neither the parents nor the guardians of political conventions" and they "cannot give legal rulings on [their] operation or scope, because those matters are determined within the political world".[48] This was so notwithstanding that the Sewel convention had been written into legislation – that legislation was taken only to recognise "the convention for

---

43   For commentary see, eg, *Khushal Murkens*, Mixed Messages in Bottles: the European Union, Devolution, and the Future of the Constitution, 80 MLR (2017), 685.

44   *R (Miller) v Secretary of State*; *In re McCord*; *In re Agnew* [2017] UKSC 5, [2018] AC 61, 161, para 130.

45   *R (Miller) v Secretary of State* [2017] UKSC 5, [2017] 2 WLR 583, 657, para 138, citing the document at note 31 above and text.

46   *R (Miller) v Secretary of State* [2017] UKSC 5, [2017] 2 WLR 583, 657-8, para 140, referencing, among others, the European Communities (Amendment) Act 2008, Wales Act 2014, the Scotland Act 2016.

47   *R (Miller) v Secretary of State* [2017] UKSC 5, [2017] UKSC 5, [2017] 2 WLR 583, paras 146 & 151.

48   *R (Miller) v Secretary of State* [2017] UKSC 5, [2017] 2 WLR 583, para 146.

what it is, namely a political convention [...] the purpose of the legislative recognition of the convention was to entrench it as a convention".[49]

The Supreme Court's ruling on this point has attracted much critical commentary, not least because it was suggestive of "power-hoarding" within the UK constitution. This is a phrase that was famously coined by *Anthony King*, who described it in terms of "a concentration – and usually a centralisation – of political power. Not only that [...] the institutions of a power-hoarding regime are associated closely with a political culture that legitimises and reinforces the hoarding of power. The guiding normative principle [...] is 'winner takes all'".[50] Of course, in the context of *Miller*, the doctrinal basis for such hoarding was a Diceyan view of Parliamentary sovereignty,[51] which shaped the Court's ruling in two related ways. The first was in its limited analysis of the status and effects of the devolution legislation in Northern Ireland, Scotland and Wales. While the Court made mention of the importance of the devolution settlement in Northern Ireland in particular, it plainly considered that the central question before it was whether the Royal prerogative had been displaced by the European Communities Act 1972. This inevitably meant that, once the Court had concluded that a further Act of the Westminster Parliament would be required to facilitate notification under Article 50 TEU, little could have been gained from considering in detail whether the devolution legislation would have also required an Act of the Westminster Parliament before notification could be given. However, to the extent that this may have had an internal logic from the point of view of Diceyan orthodoxy, it missed the point that the devolution legislation had earlier been recognised as having a constitutional status that corresponded with localised democratic processes. The ruling, in that sense, marked a quiet retreat from the promise of *Robinson*, *Axa*, and *Recovery of Medical Costs*.

The second way was in the Court's treatment of the Sewel convention, which, in effect, rejected any idea that there might be a "divided sovereignty" within the UK. The contrary approach would have required the Court to regard the Sewel convention as having legal consequences, where an entry point may have been found in the statement that judges can recognise the operation of a political convention when deciding a legal question – it having

---

49   *R (Miller) v Secretary of State* [2017] UKSC 5, [2017] 2 WLR 583, paras 148-9.

50   See *King*, Does the United Kingdom still have a constitution?, 2001, pp. 9–10. See also his use of the imagery in id., The British Constitution, 2007.

51   See *Ewing*, Brexit and Parliamentary Sovereignty, 80 Modern Law Review (2017),711.

been suggested in commentary that this would require judges to form an anterior view about the nature and scope of the relevant convention.[52] However, this may be precisely where the orthodoxy of the Supreme Court's ruling was at its most apparent, as the Court may well have already formed just such a view when vouchsafing the UK Parliament's powers. The point here is that the Court clearly envisaged only a subordinate constitutional role for the devolved legislatures, where it limited that role by tying the Sewel convention to a bright-line distinction between the realms of law and politics. Moreover, to the extent that the Court had earlier reasserted the UK Parliament's sovereign authority in respect of the prerogative, it was perhaps inevitable that the Court would regard the realm of law as synonymous with that same authority. The result was that the European Union (Notification of Withdrawal) Act 2017 was to be enacted without any Sewel motions having been passed and for notification on foot of that Act to be given on 29 March 2017.

D. Legislating for the domestic law effects of Brexit

The next challenge for the devolution settlement arose in the context of legislating for the domestic law effects of withdrawal from the EU. While the vote of 23 June 2016 had constituted a UK-wide popular/political choice to leave the EU, the domestic legal mechanisms for doing so were, and remain, highly complicated. At source, this has been a challenge about what to do, post-Brexit, with the body of EU law that has had legal effects under the European Communities Act 1972 but which will no longer be underpinned by that enabling legislation. For the UK government, the stated priority has been to ensure that there will be legal certainty and continuity on the statute book, whilst recognising that the central and devolved institutions will in time wish to amend the law in accordance with their own policy preferences.[53] However, this approach has given rise to the question of whether the devolved institutions should be able to develop devolved policies in areas that were governed by EU law from the very moment of Brexit, or whether

---

52   *Elliott*, The Supreme Court's Ruling in *Miller*: In Search of Constitutional Principle, 76 Cambridge Law Journal (2017), 257, 276-7.

53   See *Legislating for the United Kingdom's Withdrawal from the European Union* 2017, Cmnd 9446, available at https://www.gov.uk/government/publications/the-repeal-bill-white-paper/legislating-for-the-united-kingdoms-withdrawal-from-the-european-union.

there should be any limitations on their capacity to do so.[54] It is a question that has revealed sharp differences of opinion as between the Scottish and UK governments and has resulted in a further Supreme Court ruling on the powers of the Scottish institutions.

The starting point for the disagreement between the Scottish and UK governments was the proposed content, and means of enactment, of the Westminster Parliament's European Union (Withdrawal) Act 2018. (The Welsh government initially also raised concerns about the Act but later recommended consent for it; no issue about consent arose in Northern Ireland because of a political impasse which has meant that its institutions have not been sitting since January 2017.)[55] The Act, which will be complemented by further UK-wide legislation in areas that include customs, trade, and immigration, governs the effects of, what it terms, "exit day".[56] Broadly speaking, the Act will have the effect of repealing the European Communities Act 1972 on that day but will keep much of EU law on the statute book as a new species of domestic law ("retained EU law") that is to be read in the light pre-Brexit rulings of the Court of Justice (where there will continue to be a link to EU law's supremacy principle) as well post-Brexit rulings of the Court of Justice (which will not be binding on the courts).[57] These provisions were criticised by some senior members of the judiciary as lacking in clarity and likely to cause confusion,[58] and concerns were also expressed about the Act's related repeal of the Charter of Fundamental Rights of the European Union (section 5) and the granting of powers to UK government Ministers to make extensive, if time-limited, use of subordinate legislation to amend the statute book (section 8).[59] The concern about the Charter was (of course) about a diminution of the protection of rights, whereas that about the use of subordinate

---

54   For the leading (early) commentary see *Rawlings*, Brexit and the Territorial Constitution: Devolution, Reregulation and Inter-governmental Relations, published by the Constitution Society at https://consoc.org.uk/wp-content/uploads/2017/10/Brexit-and-devolution-final-2.pdf.

55   On the constitutional implications of the impasse – which is ongoing at the time of writing – see *Re Buick* [2018] NICA 26, as read in the light of the Northern Ireland (Executive Formation and Exercise of Functions) Act 2018.

56   Section 20. On the related legislation see the text of the Queen's Speech of 2017, available at https://www.gov.uk/government/speeches/queens-speech-2017.

57   Sections 1-7 and 20.

58   Irish Legal News, Lady Hale outlines concerns with language of Brexit bill, 22 March 2018, available at http://www.irishlegal.com/11809/lady-hale-outlines-concerns-language-brexit-bill/.

59   Note that the time-limit for use of the powers under section 8 is two-years from exit day (section 8(8)). On these provisions, and the Act more generally, see *Elliott*

legislation fastened upon the quality of democratic scrutiny and control.[60] In the particular context of devolution, the section 8 power was also criticised for the reason it could potentially be used in areas of devolved comptetence, where section 11 of, and Schedule 2, to the Act, similarly empower the devolved institutions to use subordinate legislation to amend the statute book in devolved areas (subject to a duty to consult UK ministers in narrowly defined circumstances)[61]. Section 12 of the Act in turn addressed the question of how far the devolved institutions would be free to develop their own policy preferences in areas that were previously governed by EU law: competence is here taken by the Act to rest at the devolved levels but UK Ministers can make subordinate legislation that freezes competence in policy areas that are said to require so-called UK-wide "common frameworks".[62]

The power to make subordinate legislation under section 12 is linked to a requirement that UK government Ministers should co-operate with their devolved counterparts and, while legislation may still be made without agreement, it was this emphasis on co-operation that led the Welsh government to recommend a Sewel motion in favour of the Act.[63] However, the position of

---

and *Tierney*, Political Pragmatism and Constitutional Principle: The European Union (Withdrawal) Act 2018, 37 Public Law (2018).

60 On rights see, eg, *Kramer* (BrexitLawNI), Brexit, The Withdrawal Agreement, and a Bill of Rights for Northern Ireland, available at http://rightsni.org/2018/02/brexit-the-withdrawal-agreement-and-a-bill-of-rights-for-northern-ireland/; and on subordinate legislation see *The Great Repeal Bill and Delegated Powers*, (note 33).

61 There is a duty to consult UK Ministers where: (1) their consent would already be required by the devolution legislation; (2) where the proposed amendments are to take effect before exit day; and (3) where the proposed amendments touch upon reciprocal arrangements between the UK and EU. See Schedule 2, paras 4-7. Note also that UK government Ministers can make amendments to the statute book under section 11 but can do so only by "acting jointly" with their devolved counterparts: Schedule 2, para 1(2).

62 On common frameworks see *Frameworks Analysis: Breakdown of areas of EU law that intersect with devolved competence in Scotland, Wales and Northern Ireland*, available at https://www.gov.uk/government/publications/frameworks-analysis. Note that the the power to make regulations under section 12 is time-limited to two-years after Brexit: see, as regards Scotland, section 30A(7) of the Scotland Act 1998. See also section 109A(8) of the Government of Wales Act 2006 and section 6A(7) of the Northern Ireland Act 1998.

63 It might be noted that the National Assembly for Wales had in fact also enacted its own withdrawal legislation – the Law Derived from the European Union (Wales) Act 2018 – but that Act was not been brought into force and has since been repealed: see https://gov.wales/topics/international/europeanaffairs/law-derived-from-the-eu-bill/?lang=en.

the Scottish government was different, as it remained of the view not only that the Act was a "power-grab" but also that the Westminster Parliament had allocated insufficient time for consideration of devolution during Parliamentary debates (which had seen the rejection of amendments that had been favoured by the party of government in Scotland, the Scottish Nationalist Party). This resulted in the Scottish government refusing to recommend a Sewel motion and introducing its own withdrawal Bill – the UK Withdrawal from the European Union (Legal Continuity) (Scotland) Bill – in the Scottish Parliament. That Bill, which was passed in advance of the enactment of the Westminster Act, sought to ensure "the effective operation of Scots law (so far as within devolved competence) upon and after UK withdrawal", where "devolved EU-derived domestic legislation [...] [will continue] to have effect in Scots law after exit day".[64] In doing so, the Bill contained a large number of provisions that sought to distinguish Scots law, and two of those can be highlighted for present purposes. The first was section 5, by which the general principles of EU law and the Charter of Fundamental Rights were to be retained in Scots law – something that would maintain a link between Scots law and the wider European fundamental rights regime. The second was section 17, which sought to protect areas of devolved competence from the wide law-making powers that were given to UK government Ministers under the European Union (Withdrawal) Act 2018. The Scottish Bill here provided that subordinate legislation made by a UK government Minister in an area that includes devolved competence could not have legal effects "unless the consent of the Scottish Ministers was obtained before [the legislation] was made, confirmed or approved".

The legality of the Bill was subsequently referred to the Supreme Court by the UK government's law officers where, as has already been noted in the introduction, the Court ruled that the Scottish Parliament's powers were greatly constrained by the terms of the Scotland Act 1998.[65] The Court's ruling in this regard was prefaced by a statement of the principles that had previously been said to govern the devolution settlement in Scotland: the Scottish Parliament's powers " are delimited by law"; the Scottish Parliament is "a democratically elected legislature with [...] plenary powers within the limits of its legislative competence [...] [but] it does not enjoy the sovereignty of the Crown in [the Westminster] Parliament"; the Scottish Parliament cannot

---

64   Sections 1-2.

65   *The UK Withdrawal from the European Union (Legal Continuity) (Scotland) Bill – A Reference by the Attorney General and the Advocate General for Scotland* [2018] UKSC 64 (note 4). The power to refer Bills to the Supreme Court that was engaged in this case is contained in section 33 of the Scotland Act 1998.

affect the power of the Westminster Parliament to make laws for Scotland; the courts must give effect to the provisions of the Scotland Act 1998; and the courts must interpret the Scotland Act 1998 in the same way as any other statute whilst having regard for "its aim to achieve a constitutional settlement and therefore recognise the importance of giving a consistent and predictable interpretation of the Scotland Act so that the Scottish Parliament has a coherent, stable and workable system within which to exercise its legislative powers".[66] When outlining these principles, the Court noted that the relevant case law had all pre-dated the impact of the Scottish independence referendum of 2014, and it thus referred to the statutory recognition that had since been given both to the permanence of the devolved institutions in Scotland and the role of the Sewel convention. On the significance of the latter, the Court referred to *Miller* and the absence of a Scottish vote in favour of the European Union (Withdrawal) Act 2018 before saying: "On this occasion [...] the Scottish Parliament voted to refuse a legislative consent motion [...]. That vote does not affect the legal validity of the UK Withdrawal Act [...] there is now a conflict between that Act and the Scottish Bill".[67]

The Supreme Court's ruling thereafter centred upon a number of questions that had been referred to it by the Law Officers and, of those, three are of particular importance to this chapter. The first was whether the Scottish Parliament had even been competent to pass the Bill or whether it had transgressed into "reserved matters" when doing so (such matters being those upon which only the Westminster Parliament can legislate).[68] According to section 29(2)(b) of the Scotland Act 1998, legislation passed by the Scottish Parliament will be outside its competence if "it relates to reserved matters", where paragraph 7 of Part 1 of Schedule 5 to the Act notes, as a reserved

---

66 *The UK Withdrawal from the European Union (Legal Continuity) (Scotland) Bill – A Reference by the Attorney General and the Advocate General for Scotland* [2018] UKSC 64, paras 12-13, citing *Whaley v Lord Watson* 2000 SC 340, 348-349, *Lord Rodger; Martin v Most* [2010] UKSC 10, 2010 SC (UKSC) 40, para 52, *Lord Walker; AXA General Insurance Ltd v Lord Advocate* [2011] UKSC 46, [2012] 1 AC 868, paras 45-46, *Lord Hope*, paras 146-147, *Lord Reed; Imperial Tobacco Ltd v Lord Advocate* 2012 SC 297, para 58, Lord Reed, [2012] UKSC 61, 2013 SC (UKSC) 153, paras 6 and 12-15, *Lord Hope; Attorney General v National Assembly for Wales Commission* [2012] UKSC 53, [2013] 1 AC 792, paras 78-81, *Lord Hope*; and *In re Agricultural Sector (Wales) Bill* [2014] UKSC 43, [2014] 1 WLR 2622, para 66, *Lords Reed and Thomas*.
67 *The UK Withdrawal from the European Union (Legal Continuity) (Scotland) Bill – A Reference by the Attorney General and the Advocate General for Scotland* [2018] UKSC 64, paras 19-20.
68 For analysis see *Page*, Constitutional Law of Scotland, 2015, ch 7.

matter, "International relations, including relations with [...] the European Union (and their institutions) and other international organisations". The Law Officers had here argued that the entirety of the Bill was outside the competence of the Scottish Parliament because, among other things, it purported to deal with relations with the EU in a manner that was specific to Scotland and which was inconsistent with Schedule 5's UK-wide approach to international relations. Rejecting that argument, the Supreme Court acknowledged the state-centric basis for international relations and that Scotland is not a "member state" but "participates in the EU as an integral part of the UK".[69] However, for the Court, the fundamental issue before it was whether the Bill could be said to "relate to" relations with the EU, as that was the test that was mandated by section 29(2)(b). Having referred to the leading case law on the meaning of that phrase, the Court concluded that the Bill did not so relate because it would "take effect at a time when there will be no legal relations with the EU unless a further treaty is made" and because it sought to regulate "the legal consequences in Scotland of the cessation of EU law as a source of domestic law relating to devolved matters, which will result from the withdrawal from the EU already authorised by the UK Parliament".[70] In the view of the Court, this was something that the Scottish Parliament was competent to do so long as the Bill otherwise remained consistent with the limitations on its powers under the Scotland Act 1998.

The second question was whether section 17 of the Bill – on the need for Scottish Ministers to consent to subordinate legislation on devolved matters that is made by UK government Ministers – was within competence. This was essentially a question about whether the Bill would modify section 28(7) of the Scotland Act 1998, which provides that nothing in that Act affects "the power of the (UK) Parliament [...] to make laws for Scotland" and which, *per* paragraph 4(1) of Schedule 4 to the Act, is "protected" from modification by the Scottish Parliament. In terms of constitutional principle, section 28(7)

---

69   *The UK Withdrawal from the European Union (Legal Continuity) (Scotland) Bill – A Reference by the Attorney General and the Advocate General for Scotland* [2018] UKSC 64, para 29.

70   *The UK Withdrawal from the European Union (Legal Continuity) (Scotland) Bill – A Reference by the Attorney General and the Advocate General for Scotland* [2018] UKSC 64, para 33. The case law to which the Court referred was *Martin v Most* [2010] UKSC 10, 2010 SC (UKSC) 40 and *Imperial Tobacco Ltd v Lord Advocate* [2012] UKSC 61, 2013 SC (UKSC) 153: see *The UK Withdrawal from the European Union (Legal Continuity) (Scotland) Bill – A Reference by the Attorney General and the Advocate General for Scotland* [2018] UKSC 64, para 27.

is where the sovereignty of the UK Parliament finds its most obvious expression in the Scotland Act 1998, and the Supreme Court stated that "That section makes it clear that [...] the UK Parliament remains sovereign, and its legislative power in relation to Scotland is undiminished".[71] The Lord Advocate, acting on behalf of the Scottish Government, had here argued that section 17 would not modify section 28(7) because it would only have implications for subordinate legislation made under an Act of Parliament and also because the UK Parliament could in any event legislate to disapply or repeal section 17. However, his submissions in this regard were all rejected for the reason that section 17 would have the effect of setting at nought those provisions of the European Union (Withdrawal) Act 2018 that allow UK ministers to make subordinate legislation. As the Court expressed the point:

> "[T]he power of the UK Parliament to make laws for Scotland includes the power to make laws authorising the making of subordinate legislation by Ministers and other persons. An enactment of the Scottish Parliament which prevented such subordinate legislation from having legal effect, unless the Scottish Ministers gave their consent, would render the effect of laws made by the UK Parliament conditional on the consent of the Scottish Ministers. It would therefore limit the power of the UK Parliament to make laws for Scotland, since Parliament cannot meaningfully be said to "make laws" if the laws which it makes are of no effect. The imposition of such a condition on the UK Parliament's law-making power would be inconsistent with the continued recognition, by section 28(7) of the Scotland Act, of its unqualified legislative power".[72]

The third question was whether the Court could consider the effects of the European Union (Withdrawal) Act 2018 given that the Bill pre-dated the enactment of the Westminster legislation. This required the Court to consider the nature of the constitutional mechanism by which the Bill had been referred to it, and it concluded, in the particular context of the reference, that the Bill should be read in the light of the Westminster Act.[73] This was a point of very real significance, as the Scotland Act 1998 had since been amended

71 *The UK Withdrawal from the European Union (Legal Continuity) (Scotland) Bill – A Reference by the Attorney General and the Advocate General for Scotland* [2018] UKSC 64, para 41.

72 *The UK Withdrawal from the European Union (Legal Continuity) (Scotland) Bill – A Reference by the Attorney General and the Advocate General for Scotland* [2018] UKSC 64, para 52.

73 *The UK Withdrawal from the European Union (Legal Continuity) (Scotland) Bill – A Reference by the Attorney General and the Advocate General for Scotland* [2018] UKSC 64, paras 91-97.

to include the European Union (Withdrawal) Act 2018 within the list of protected legislation that is contained in Schedule 4 to the Scotland Act 1998. As noted above, the inclusion of legislation in that Schedule protects it from modification by the Scottish Parliament, and the Court thus conducted an audit of the Bill to assess which provisions would modify the Westminster Act and thereby be beyond the competence of the Scottish Parliament.[74] The offending provisions were said to include, among many others, section 5 on the contined effect to the general principles of EU law and the Charter of Fundamental Rights of the European Union – this was an "inconsistency" that would "clearly" amount to a modification of European Union (Withdrawal) Act 2018 and "therefore would not be law".[75]

It would appear from the Court's ruling on these questions that the devolution case law has now settled upon a resolutely non-federal model of sovereignty. While there were certainly aspects of the ruling that drew upon the Court's earlier reasoning in *Axa* and so on – the Court emphasised again that the Scottish Parliament has full plenary powers within the limits of the Scotland Act 1998[76] – the judgment ultimately rested upon the Diceyan model of sovereignty that had informed *Miller*. This could be seen not just in the Court's approach to the effects of the absence of a Sewel motion, but also in its various references to the sovereignty of the UK Parliament, as takes form in section 28(7) of the Scotland Act 1998. Indeed, at paragraph 41 of its judgment, the Court, when discussing that section, said that: "It reflects the essence of devolution: in contrast to a federal model, a devolved system preserves the powers of the central legislature of the state in relation to all matters, whether devolved or reserved". Given the point, it might well be doubted whether *Lord Thomas'* earlier comments in *Welsh Asbestos Diseases* will ever amount to anything more than a statement of ambition rather than of constitutional principle.

---

74 *The UK Withdrawal from the European Union (Legal Continuity) (Scotland) Bill – A Reference by the Attorney General and the Advocate General for Scotland* [2018] UKSC 64, paras 98-124.

75 *The UK Withdrawal from the European Union (Legal Continuity) (Scotland) Bill – A Reference by the Attorney General and the Advocate General for Scotland* [2018] UKSC 64, para 102.

76 See variously *The UK Withdrawal from the European Union (Legal Continuity) (Scotland) Bill – A Reference by the Attorney General and the Advocate General for Scotland* [2018] UKSC 64, paras 11, 35, and 86.

E.   *Northern Ireland and the Belfast Agreement*

The remaining matter to be addressed is that of Northern Ireland and whether Brexit can be achieved in a manner that will safeguard the Belfast/Good Friday Agreement of 1998.[77] That Agreement famously provided the basis for devolution after a protracted period of violent conflict in Northern Ireland, and it is premised upon a number of "values" that have been said to have a constitutional status under the Northern Ireland Act 1998.[78] Legally speaking, this is the realm of the *Robinson* case that was referred to above, in which the House of Lords (now Supreme Court) interpreted the Northern Ireland Act 1998 purposively so as to bolster the devolved institutions and, by extension, the Northern Irelandpeace process.[79] The corresponding importance of the Belfast/Good Friday Agreement has since been underlined by the UK-government and the EU-27 during the Brexit negotiations, where there has been a shared concern to avoid a "hard border" on the island of Ireland. However, achieving that outcome in practice has proven challenging, and controversial proposals for a customs "backstop" – contained in the Withdrawal Agreement of November 2018 that was overwhelmingly rejected in an initial vote in the UK's House of Commons[80] – have become central to the possibility of a "no deal" Brexit. For some, a Brexit in that form could only ever unravel much of what the Belfast/Good Friday Agreement embodies.[81]

---

[77]   See further *Anthony*, Brexit and the Irish Border: Legal and Political Questions' Royal Irish Academy – British Academy Brexit Briefing, October 2017, available at https://www.thebritishacademy.ac.uk/sites/default/files/BrexitandtheIrishBorderLegalandPoliticalQuestions.pdf.

[78]   The Agreement, in its original terms, is available at https://www.gov.uk/government/publications/the-belfast-agreement. For early analysis see *Harvey* (ed.), (note 9). On the conflict see *McKittrick et al*, Lost Lives: The Stories of the Men, Women and Children Who Died as a Result of the Troubles, 1999.

[79]   *Robinson v Secretary of State for Northern Ireland* [2002] UKHL 32, [2002] NI 390. For commentary see *Morison* and *Lynch*, Litigating the Agreement: Towards a New Judicial Constitutionalism for the UK from Northern Ireland, in: Morison, McEvoy and Anthony (eds.), Judges, Transition and Human Rights: Essays in Memory of Stephen Livingstone, 2008, ch 7.

[80]   BBC News, Brexit: Theresa May's deal is voted down in historic commons defeat, 15 January 2019, https://www.bbc.com/news/uk-politics-46885828.

[81]   See, eg, *Harvey*, Sharing the Island: Brexit, "No Deal" and the Constitutional Future, available at https://brexitlawni.org/blog/sharing-the-island-brexit-no-deal-and-the-constitutional-future/. Note that there have been efforts to use procedures within the UK Parliament to prevent or at the least frustrate the prospect of a "no

Broadly speaking, the Belfast/Good Friday Agreement can best be under-stood in terms of institutional relationships not just in Northern Ireland itself but also on the island of Ireland as whole and as between Ireland and the UK. While the devolved institutions of course offer the immediate point of comparison with Scotland and Wales – albeit an ongoing political impasse means that the Northern Ireland institutions are not sitting at present[82] – their role is to be understood with reference to two other institutions envisaged by the Belfast/Good Friday Agreement. The first is the North/South Ministerial Council (N/SMC) that was established by the British and Irish governments and which brings together Ministers from Northern Ireland and Ireland for cooperation on matters of mutual interest.[83] While the N/SMC does not have any executive powers, the Belfast Agreement provides that its meetings should enable "those with executive responsibilities [...] to develop consultation, cooperation and action within the island of Ireland [...] on matters of mutual interest within the competence of the Administrations, North and South" and that it should "consider the EU dimension of relevant matters, including the implementation of EU policies and programmes [...] Arrangements [are] to be made to ensure that the views of the [N/SMC] are taken into account and represented appropriately at relevant EU meetings".[84] The second institution is the British-Irish Council (BIC), which is a discussion forum that brings together representatives of the UK and Irish Governments, the three devolved executives, and the governments of the Isle of Man and the Channel Islands so that they might "promote the harmonious and mutually beneficial development of the totality of relationships among the peoples of these islands".[85] While the BIC has not been as a prominent an institution as

---

deal" Brexit: see BBC News, Brexit: MPs try to limit government's no deal financial powers, 8 January 2019, available at https://www.bbc.co.uk/news/uk-politics-46789565.

82   See note 55 above.

83   The text of the Belfast Agreement had two related parts: a multi-party agreement between the political parties in Northern Ireland; and an intergovernmental agreement known as the British-Irish Agreement, which was an annex to the multi-party agreement. While the N/SMC was mentioned in the multi-party agreement, the duty to establish it was imposed upon the two governments under Article 2 of the British-Irish Agreement (which also obliged the governments to create a number of North/South Implementation Bodies that would work under the N/SMC).

84   *Belfast Agreement, Agreement reached in the multi-party negotiations*, Strand two, paras 1 & 17.

85   *Belfast Agreement, Agreement reached in the multi-party negotiations*, Strand three, 'British–Irish Council', para 1. Note that the duty to create the BIC was

the N/SMC, it has provided an important East-West dimension to the Belfast Agreement and has since also been said to have played something of a role in normalising British–Irish relations[86] (where there is a British–Irish Inter-governmental Confererence that brings together "the British and Irish Governments to promote bilateral co-operation at all levels on matters of mutual interest within the competence of both Governments"[87]). As with the N/SMC, the Belfast/Good Friday Agreement envisaged that the BIC might provide a forum for discussing EU law as a matter of shared interest and for formulating agreed policies.[88]

The values that underlie these relationships start with a meta-value, or "principle", of consent.[89] The fundamental purpose of that principle is to accommodate competing ethno-national aspirations in Northern Ireland by recognising (i) that Northern Ireland is a part of the UK but that (ii) it will form a part of a United Ireland should that become the expressed wish of the majority of its electorate and that in Ireland (the Belfast/Good Friday Agreement itself having been endorsed by parallel *referenda* in Northern Ireland and Ireland).[90] This is the foundation stone for devolution in Northern Ireland, where its constitutional status is taken as contingent rather than fixed, and where changes were made to the Irish Constitution of 1937 to recognise the complexity of Northern Ireland's position.[91] The basis for devolution is, moreover, tied to much more than just a bare majoritarian preference about that position, as the consent principle intersects with a range of other values

---

imposed upon the UK and Irish governments under Article 2 of the British-Irish Agreement at note 83 above. The leading commentary on the BIC remains *Bogdanor*, The British–Irish Council and Devolution, 34 *Government and Opposition* (1999), 287.

86   *Coakley*, British Irish Institutional Structures: Towards a New Relationship, 29 Irish Political Studies (2014), 76.

87   *Belfast Agreement, Agreement reached in the multi-party negotiations*, Strand three, 'British-Irish Intergovernmental Conference', para 2.

88   *Belfast Agreement, Agreement reached in the multi-party negotiations*, Strand three, 'British–Irish Council', para 5; and Northern Ireland Act 1998, Sch 2, para 3(b).

89   See *MacGinty et al*, Consenting Adults: The Principle of Consent and Northern Ireland's Constitutional Futures, 36 Government and Opposition (2001), 472.

90   *Belfast Agreement, Annex, British–Irish Agreement*, 'Constitutional Issues'; Northern Ireland Act 1998, s 1; and Irish Constitution of 1937, Article 3. On the potential for, and implications of, Irish unification see *Humphreys*, Countdown to Unity: Debating Irish Reunification, 2008, and *Humphreys*, Beyond the Border: The Good Friday Agreement and Irish Unity After Brexit, 2018.

91   Viz, Articles 2 & 3 of the Irish Constitution. See further *Anthony*, (note 77).

and principles that characterise the very essence of the Belfast Agreement.[92] They include values of mutual recognition and political equality; a commitment to power-sharing/consociationalism; commitments about the protection of fundamental rights; and the development of the above-mentioned North/South and East–West institutional relationships. Relevant, too, are commitments about citizenship: those born on the island of Ireland are entitled to claim either Irish and/or British citizenship where there are, in turn, the attendant rights of European citizenship.[93]

Plainly, a "no deal" Brexit would cut across these arrangments in a number of ways.[94] The first would be by complicating the narrative around the interlocking institutional relationships that were established by the Belfast/Good Friday Agreement. Although the text of the Belfast/Good Friday Agreement mentions the fact of joint UK and Irish membership of the EU only a few times, this is because membership had been taken as an ongoing reality that had conditioned debates about, among other things, economic cooperation, citizenship and sovereignty.[95] Of course, the most obvious way in which "no deal" would affect that narrative would be in the context of areas of economic activity, where a "hard border" with customs checks could be expected and where a creep towards different regulatory regimes would be almost inevitable.[96] However, the implications of "no deal" go beyond economics and include, for instance, issues related to the protection of fundamental rights. While the Belfast/Good Friday Agreement made a primary link between the ECHR and the protection of rights, there are large areas of law in which the EU has been a harbinger of rights standards, most notably in the area of non-

---

92   See further *O'Leary*, The Nature of the Agreement, 22 Fordham International Law Journal (1999), 1628.

93   *Belfast Agreement, Agreement reached in the multi-party negotiations*, 'Constitutional Issues', para 1(vi) and *Annex: Agreement between the Government of the United Kingdom of Great Britain and Northern Ireland the Government of Ireland*, Article 1(vi). But note also the controversy that surrounded the Twenty-Seventh Amendment of the Irish Constitution – see *Mullally*, Defining the limits of citizenship: family life, immigration and "non-nationals" in Irish law, Irish Jurist (2004), 334.

94   On Parliamenary efforts to frustrate a no deal Brexit see note 81 above.

95   For context see *Meehan*, Europe and the Europeanisation of the Irish question, in Cox, Guelke and Stephen (eds.), A Farewell to Arms? Beyond the Good Friday Agreement, 2nd edn, 2006, ch 22.

96   On some of the questions see *Dougan*, The "Brexit" Threat to the Northern Irish Border: Clarifying the Constitutional Framework, in Dougan (ed.), The UK After Brexit: Legal and Policy Challenges, 2017, p. 53.

discrimination.[97] Even though the European Union (Withdrawal) Act 2018 envisages the (initial) retention of many of the applicable standards, a "no deal" Brexit would mean that those standards would become subject in their entirety to domestic legal preferences. That is a position that might well come to undermine the place that rights have occupied in post-conflict Northern Ireland.

The Ireland-Northern Ireland Protocol to the Withdrawal Agreement of November 2018 – which is to be read alongside the Political Declaration on Future Relations – attempts to avert such outcomes.[98] As is well-known, the Withdrawal Agreement addresses the UK's financial liabilities and the rights of UK and EU citizens, and it also envisages a transition period to the end of 2020 that will facilitate further negotiations on future EU-UK trading relations. In terms of Northern Ireland, the Preamble to the Protocol notes that its purpose is to, among other things, protect the Belfast/Good Friday Agreement "in all its parts", where Article 1 of the Protocol states that the Protocol is to be "without prejudice to the provisions of the [Belfast] Agreement regarding the constitutional status of Northern Ireland and the principle of consent", and where Article 4 obliges the UK to ensure that there shall be "no diminution of rights [...] [resulting] from its withdrawal from the Union, including in the area of discrimination as enshrined in" EU law.[99] The Protocol also affirms both parties' commitment to protecting North-South cooperation and the "guarantee" of avoiding a "hard border", and it is this commitment that underlies the controversial customs "backstop" that was mentioned above. While the Withdrawal Agreement envisages further talks on trade within the transition period – which period can be extended for up to two years[100] – Article 6 of the Protocol provides that, in the absence of a further agreement by July 2020, a single customs territory that covers all of the UK and the EU will be established and will remain in place "until the future relationship becomes applicable". Article 7 of the Protocol thereafter provides

---

97   See further *Anthony*, "Britain Alone" – A View from Northern Ireland, in: Biondi and Birkinshaw (eds.), Britain Alone: The Implications and Consequences of UK Exit from the EU, 2016, p. 57, at pp. 66-70.

98   The Draft Agreement and the Political Declaration are both available at https://www.gov.uk/government/publications/withdrawal-agreement-and-political-declaration.

99   For analysis of the Draft Agreement's provisions on rights see *McCrudden*, Brexit, Rights, and the Ireland-Northern Ireland Protocol to the Withdrawal Agreement, British Academy – Royal Irish Academy paper, available at https://www.thebritishacademy.ac.uk/publications/ europe-futures-brexit-rights-ireland-northern-ireland-protocol-withdrawal-agreement.

100   Withdrawal Agreement, Article 132.

that goods produced in Northern Ireland should continue to have "unfettered market access" to the rest of the UK's internal market, albeit the remainder of the Protocol makes it clear that there is scope for the emergence of different regulatory regimes as between Northern Ireland and Great Britain. This is the result of the requirement that Northern Irish law should track a wide range of rules for the "single market", whereas the Protocol contains no such formal requirement for the rest of the UK. Indeed, while it is true that the Protocol seeks to ensure that there is a "level playing field" throughout the customs territory – Annex 4 to the Protocol contains commitments in areas that include competition, state aid, and taxation – it is envisaged that Northern Ireland will have a unique link to the EU part of that customs territory. *Per* Article 20 of the Protocol, the backstop can be brought to an end only by the EU and UK acting jointly within the mechanisms envisaged by the Withdrawal Agreement.

The corresponding criticisms of the backstop have centred upon two main points. The first is that the customs arrangement is not time-limited, where legal advice from the UK's Attorney-General was taken to confirm that the UK would not be able to bring the backstop to an end unilaterally, even if it is only meant to operate "until the future relationship becomes applicable".[101] This led to the concern among some "Brexiteers" that the UK would be indefinitely tied to a customs arrangement that could only ever limit the UK's capacity to enter into trade deals at a global level – a capacity that Brexit was meant to guarantee.[102] The second criticism, in turn, was more Northern Ireland specific and focused on the potential for regulatory divergence as between Northern Ireland and the rest of the UK. While there were broad statements of support for the Withdrawal Agreement from within, among others, the agricultural and business sectors in Northern Ireland, the dominant unionist politicial party (the Democratic Unionist Party) consistently expressed strong opposition to the backstop.[103] Its primary concern was that the "backstop" would place Northern Ireland at one remove from the rest of the UK

---

101   The advice is available at https://www.gov.uk/government/publications/ exiting-the-eu-publication -of-legal-advice. And see, eg, The Guardian, Brexit legal advice warns of UK being trapped by Irish backstop, 5 December 2018, available at https://www.theguardian.com/politics/2018 /dec/05/brexit-legal-advice-warns-of-uk-trapped-in-talks-by-irish-backstop.

102   The Independent, Brexit: Tory eurosceptics claim legal advice paper confirms their worst fears on Theresa May's deal, 3 December 2018, available at https://www.independent.co.uk/news/uk/politics/brexit-legal   -advice-papertheresa-may-deal-conservatives-tory-party-a8665161.html.

and, in doing so, undermine its position as an integral part of the UK, Article 1 of the Protocol notwithstanding.[104] The concern, in other words, was about the emergence of a regulatory framework with a dynamic that could only move Northern Ireland closer to a United Ireland.

At the time of writing, it appears unlikely that the Withdrawal Agreement of November 2018 will be able to provide the basis for an orderly Brexit. Certainly, opposition to it grew significantly at Westminster and, as was noted above, the House of Commons voted by an overwhelming majority on 15 January 2019 to reject it.[105] That said, there were many countervailing reasons for that vote, as some so-called "remainers" voted against the Withdrawal Agreement in the hope of facilitating other outcomes, including a further referendum on membership and/or the terms of a deal.[106] However, pending clarity on the effects of the Commons' vote – which may result in further negotiations about a Withdrawal Agreement, additional Parliamentary votes, and/or a further referendum – Northern Ireland's constitutional reference points are becoming increasingly unstable. Indeed, while Northern Ireland will (of course) remain a part of the UK in the immediate aftermath of Brexit, the manner in which EU withdrawal is achieved may only open up a whole series of new debates about its constitutional future(s).[107] It is a point that will be all the more true if "no deal" becomes synonymous with a diminution of the very values that have defined the Belfast/Good Friday Agreement.

---

103   On the views of business see, eg, BBC News Northern Ireland, Brexit deal critics "should offer alternative plan", 29 November 2018, available at https://www.bbc.co.uk/news/uk-northern-ireland-46392844.

104   See Belfast Telegraph, DUP say backstop the "poison" in the Brexit deal, 6 January 2019, available at https://www.belfasttelegraph.co.uk/ news/northern-ireland/dup-says-backstop-the-poison-in-brexit-deal-37684779.html.

105   See note 80 above.

106   On a referendum see, eg, *Grieve QC MP*, Parliament is incapable of settling Brexit. We need a second referendum, The Guardian, 29 December 2018, available at https://www.theguardian.com/commentisfree/2018/dec/29/ parliament-brexit-second-referendum-eu-deal; and *The Insitute For Government*, How would a second referendum on Brexit happen?, available at https://www.instituteforgovernment.org.uk/explainers/second-referendum-brexit.

107   For this possibility see *Humphreys*, (note 89); and *Anthony*, Sovereignty, Consent and Constitutions, (note 5).

F.   Conclusion

This chapter began by noting that the title for this collection – *"Brexit, and What it Means"* – is a play on words that provides a bridging point to the very real complexities of UK withdrawal from the EU. In the subsequent pages, it examined three issues of immediate relevance to the UK's devolution settlement: the Sewel convention and whether devolved consent was required for notification under Article 50 TEU; legislative competence and whether the devolved institutions could pre-emptively legislate for the effects of EU withdrawal; and the complications that Brexit presents for the Belfast/Good Friday Agreement and devolution in Northern Ireland. The first two of these issues resulted in the Supreme Court's rulings in *Miller* and the *Scottish Withdrawal Bill Reference*, where a Diceyan model of legal sovereignty was reaffirmed as the basis for devolution, notwithstanding earlier judicial pronoucements about its limited explanatory worth.[108] The issue of the Belfast/Good Friday Agreement in turn provided an illustratration of what Diceyan sovereignty can mean in practice: the constitutional values of the Belfast/Good Friday Agreement are subject to whatever happens in the sovereign Westminster Parliament, including, potentially, a failure to legislate to give effect to a Withdrawal Agreement that seeks to protect the Belfast/Good Friday Agreement "in all its parts".

Of course, at one level, it may be misleading to focus too much on the implications of a shift towards Diceyan legal sovereignty under the UK constitution, as much of what is happening with Brexit is intrinsically political, rather than legal, in form. However, it has also been argued in other settings that constitutional law can best be understood as the "third order of the political", in the sense that it ultimately moderates disputes that are political in nature.[109] If that is what is happening under the UK constitution at present, then a move back towards Diceyan sovereignty may well prove to be more problematic in the short-to-medium term. As was noted in the introduction to this chapter, there were different "national" votes at the time of the EU referendum, in that Scotland and Northern Ireland voted to remain, and by some margins. In the subsequent debates about the form that Brexit should take, the national complexities of the EU referendum have plainly been given only a limited weight in a context where judicial reasoning has safeguarded

---

108   See, eg, *Jackson v Attorney-General* [2005] UKHL 56, [2006] 1 AC 262, 302, para 102, *Lord Styen*.

109   For such ideas see *Louglin*, Constitutional Law: The Third Order of the Political, in: Bamforth and Leyland (eds.), Public Law in a Multi-Layered Constitution, 2003, p 27.

the powers of the UK's central institutions. While it is possible that there may be a further referendum on EU membership and that that may result in a vote to remain (or to endorse something akin to the Withdrawal Agreement), there is now also the very real prospect that Brexit will take the form of a "no deal" departure. Should that occur, it has already been acknowledged in political dispatches that this could give rise to increased nationalist pressure in Scotland and Northern Ireland and a resultant break-up of the UK.[110] A Brexit of that kind, or which has that effect, could surely be synonymous with only a hastened constitutional rupture.

---

110 The Express, End of UK? Scottish independence support soars amid no deal Brexit fears, 9 December 2018, available at https://www.express.co.uk/news/politics/1056515/scotland-uk-independence-brexit-deal-poll-theresa-may-commons-vote; and Belfast Telegraph, Ministers discussed possibility of Irish border poll in event of deal Brexit – reports, 9 January 2019, available at https://www.belfasttelegraph.co.uk/news/northern-ireland/ministers-discussed-possibility-of-irish-border-poll-in-event-of-nodeal-brexit-reports-37696467.html.

Brexit, EU Citizenship, free movement of persons and the impact on Eastern Europe(ans)

Christoph Schewe

A.   Introduction

In various of the Member States from the North-East that acceded the European Union in 2004 (EU8[1]) – particularly in the Baltic States – the night of the 23 to 24 June for *St. John's day* (also known as *Jaanipäev, Jāņi, Līgo* or midsummer) is among the most popular dates of the year to celebrate. On 23 of June, people gather around bonfires to dance, sing traditional songs and feast which explains why those who live abroad are particularly fond of travelling home for these celebrations. In 2016, however, when waking up the morning after these celebrations, for those who had travelled to their home country from their new homes in the UK, reality might have had an extremely sobering effect: The British voters had voted for Brexit! Even though nobody had a clear picture of the precise implications, it became clear that consequences might indeed be sobering. Particularly given the fact that one of the Brexiteers' foremost priorities was directed against immigration from Eastern Europe, it must have been difficult for Eastern Europeans not to take the result of the referendum personally.

Today, more than two years later, the potential impact and consequences of Brexit have been extensively discussed in the media and on a scholarly level. Politicians, however, who have been negotiating since then have not (yet) succeeded to conclude an agreement that might provide the clarity for those who had moved from Eastern Europe to the UK and are worried about their future status. But the corresponding modalities are not only important for EU/UK citizens living abroad. Brexit might also have an impact on the credibility of the whole concept of EU citizenship, if – in the worst case of an unordered Brexit – the corresponding rights would not entitle EU citizens

---

1   The abbreviation EU8 is used for the Czech Republic, Estonia, Hungary, Latvia, Lithuania, Poland, Slovenia and Slovakia that acceded in 2004 in the course of the fifth enlargement of the EU.

who had taken the decision to build their lives on these rights, to remain in their country of residence.

The present contribution briefly explains the historic and political context that had an impact on the emigration of more than 1,7 million people from the EU8 and EU2[2] to the UK (B.I.), before analysing the relevance of the legal aspects on free movement for persons (B. II.). Finally, it will discuss these findings in the context of EU citizenship (B.III.).

B. Brexit, free movement of persons, Eastern Europe(ans) and the concept of EU Citizenship

One of the main aspects that played a role in the Brexit campaigns[3] was the claim for regaining control over immigration, which relatively clearly addressed immigration from Eastern Europe. While populism and migration also have become sensitive issues in most other EU Member States, migration from Eastern Europe was particularly controversial in the UK.

The background is to be seen in the UK-specific developments which might best be illustrated with corresponding numbers and statistics. Prior 2000, approx. 400.000 persons immigrated to the UK from the EU14 and around 182.000 from the EU8.[4] The situation, however, changed considerably after 2000, when the number of persons emigrating to the UK from the EU14 amounted to 474.000 while the number of persons from the EU8 almost quintupled to 932.000. In 2016 the ONS counted total immigration from

---

2   The abbreviation EU2 is used for Bulgaria and Romania that acceded in 2007 in the sixth enlargement of the EU.

3   More extensively on these aspects: *Armstrong,* Brexit Time: Leaving the EU – Why, How and When?, 2017, p. 73; and *Schewe/Lipsens*, From EFTA to EC/EU and Back to EFTA? The European Economic Area (EEA) as a Possible Scenario for the UK-EU Relations After Brexit, in: *Troitiño/Kerikmäe/Chochia* (Eds.), Brexit – History, Reasoning and Perspectives, 2018, p. 215.

4   Numbers differ in the various sources. Despite variations they however display migration over the years that played a role for the Brexit referendum. The data used in this article is taken from the *Office for National Statistics* (*ONS*), https://www.ons.gov.uk/, last accessed 4 February 2019, like all online material cited in this article; more extensively on the situation in the UK in 2016: *Armstrong,* see note 3, pp. 74-78.

the EU to 3.3 million. Among these migrants 1,3 million came from the EU8[5] and over 413.000 from the EU2,[6] contrasting UK-EU emigration of only 1.2 million persons.

Various factors have contributed to generating this effect which partially differs from other EU Member States like for instance Germany.[7] An important aspect is to be seen in the development in Europe in the past century and the reasons that led to the enlargements of 2004, 2007 and 2013. Furthermore, also other not necessarily enlargement-specific amendments and projects of the EU had a considerable impact on the further developments.

I.   Eastern Europe, the European Union and the UK

European integration and the EU's development have been considerably influenced by Europe's history – an aspect which also applies to the political Europe of the last decades of the past century and the events leading to the fifth and sixth enlargements. At this time, the division of East and West largely governed the political atmosphere and history of Europe, which still is most practically illustrated with *Winston Churchills* famous metaphor of an *iron curtain* dividing Europe. Accordingly, hopes were high when the Soviet Union (USSR) had collapsed in 1989 and chances arouse for overcoming the division of Europe. In the political debates that followed the dissolution of the USSR, it relatively early became a topic to open the EU integration process for the states that had regained their independence. In the controversy, how this could be achieved, the proponents of an enlargement of the EU to the East emphasized that an enlargement would bring enormous benefits to all: Peace, freedom, security and prosperity. The collapse of the USSR thus indeed led to a – probably – unique historic opportunity to unite Europe despite the related risks. Simultaneously, critics had highlighted considerable

---

5   Data according to the *ONS*),: https://www.ons.gov.uk/peoplepopulationandcommunity/populationandmigration/internationalmigration/articles/livingabroad/migrationbetweenbritainandtheeu8.

6   Data according to the *ONS*, https://www.ons.gov.uk/peoplepopulationandcommunity/populationandmigration/internationalmigration/articles/livingabroad/dynamicsofmigrationbetweenbritainandtheeu2.

7   *Bundesamt für Migration und Flüchtlinge,* Freizügigkeitsmonitoring: Bericht für das Jahr 2017, 04.10.2018, http://www.bamf.de/SharedDocs/Anlagen/DE/Publikationen/Broschueren/freizuegigkeitsmonitoring-jahresbericht-2017.pdf?__blob=publicationFile.

obstacles to integration, such as massive economic disparities and the prior ideological divide that had not only affected systems but also left their marks on minds, society and culture. Eventually, proponents had prevailed and the year 2004 brought an enlargement of the EU, unprecedented regarding the number of people, of acceding Member States and regarding the challenges resulting from the different levels of economic development.[8] While the enlargement strategy tried to consider these objections, it remained controversial, in how far the EU and the social systems of Member States would require specific measures, as the immediate attribution of the fundamental economic freedoms to the new EU citizens might lead to mass migration while overburdening the labour markets of other Member States.[9]

In this context, it is noteworthy that during the time of the 2004 enlargement, three major EU projects coincided: firstly, the enlargement, secondly, the drafting of the services directive[10], and thirdly, the endeavours to a *Treaty establishing a Constitution for Europe* (*Constitutional Treaty*). Critics sensed a neo-liberalist orientation, which might weaken the social achievements that reflected in the Member States' structures. Particularly the initial concept of the European Commission's proposal of the services directive that stipulated the "principle of origin" for services providers[11] was heavily criticized for disturbing the social-economic balance in Member States.[12] At the same time, critics suspected that the *Constitutional Treaty* might provide the additional legal framework for this shift.[13] Accordingly, some regarded the three political projects not independently but as a neo-liberal strategy exercising pressure on employment, salaries and working conditions in old Member

---

8   *Lazowski*, The Application of EU Law in the New Member States: Brave New World, 2010, pp. 7-28.

9   This contribution will not comment on the challenges for economic and political systems in the EU8 Member States which also (might have) deserved particular sensitivity and attention.

10 Services in the Internal Market Directive 2006/123/EC, OJ 2006 L376/36.

11 *Fichtner*, The Rise and Fall of the Country of Origin Principle, Uncovering the Principle's Premises and Implications, in: Beiträge zum Transnationalen Wirtschaftsrecht 2006, Heft 54, http://telc.jura.uni-halle.de/sites/default/files/alt-bestand/Heft54.pdf.

12 For instance *Attac*, mobilising against the "Bolkenstein directive" in 2005, http://attac.de/archive/Bolkestein/www.attac.de/bolkestein/.

13 *Hainsworth*, France Says No: The 29 May 2005 Referendum on the European Constitution, Parliamentary Affairs, Volume 59, Issue 1, 1 January 2006, 98, 104.

States. Subsequently, these suspicions became central in campaigns that influenced the outcome of the referenda held in the Netherlands and France which signified the failure of the *Constitutional Treaty*. In parallel, continuous political resistance against the services directive contributed to considerable modifications of the original proposal of the European Commission.[14] Furthermore, responding to the fears of mass migration of Eastern European workers to the labour markets, most Member States negotiated transitional periods with restrictions for workers from the EU8.[15]

Despite these restrictions, accession to the EU brought an unprecedented freedom to move and to exercise previously inexistent economic freedoms for the citizens of the EU8. In contrast to the restrictions of most Member States, the UK, Ireland and Sweden, however, had adopted a different approach and immediately opened their labour markets to the citizens of the new Member States. Accordingly, those from the EU8 who wanted to seize the new opportunities in the EU focussed on these three Member States which explains the extent of migration to the UK after 2004. As a result, in 2016 approx. 1.3 million persons from the EU8 resided in the UK,[16] making use of their rights granted by Art. 45 TFEU and Art. 21 TFEU. In addition, 413.000 citizens from the EU2 resided in the UK.[17] While these developments became one of the main issues in the Brexit campaign, the correspond-

---

14   See note 11.

15   *European Commission*, Free movement: workers from eight Member States that joined EU in 2004 finally enjoy full rights, Press Release, IP/11/506, 28 April 2011, http://europa.eu/rapid/press-release_IP-11-506_en.htm; *ibid*, The end of transitional arrangements for the free movement of workers on 30 April 2011, MEMO/11/259, 28 April 2011, http://europa.eu/rapid/press-release_MEMO-11-259_en.htm.

16   *ONS* regarding EU8, see note 5.

17   *ONS* regarding EU2, see note 6; in this regard it is noteworthy that the European Commission had believed that migration would remain relatively low, see: *European Commission*, Free movement: workers from eight Member States that joined EU in 2004 finally enjoy full rights, Press Release, IP/11/506, 28 April 2011, http://europa.eu/rapid/press-release_IP-11-506_en.htm.

ing Member States of origin increasingly face demographic problems partially resulting from migration, an aspect which will, however, not be addressed in this article.[18]

Apart from Brexit, it is noteworthy that, despite the failure of the Constitutional Treaty, the modifications of the services directive and the transitional phase, these concerns still persist also in other Member States and people remain sensitive to these issues while politicians continuously refer to these or related matters.[19]

II. Free movement of persons after Brexit

Art. 50 (3) TEU stipulates that

> "[...]The Treaties shall cease to apply to the State in question from the date of entry into force of the withdrawal agreement or, failing that, two years after the notification referred to in paragraph 2, unless the European Council [...] decides to extend this period."

This implies that – unless a Withdrawal Agreement (WA) is signed and enters into force at a specified date – from 29 March 2019 on, the citizens who have used their corresponding rights of free movement would depend on the corresponding national law. For UK citizens in the EU the potential loss of privileges has been illustrated with an "Argentinisation of British citizenship".[20] Likewise, the citizens from the EU would lose the rights to remain in the UK and thus depend on national rules for foreigners.

In order to avoid these consequences, the UK and EU principally agreed in a Joint Report (JR) that they would strive "*to provide reciprocal protection*

---

18 Today, 14 years after the enlargement the EU8/EU2 have to cope with the consequences of emigration, see for instance the studies by the *IMF,* Emigration and Its Economic Impact on Eastern Europe, July 2016, https://www.imf.org/external/pubs/ft/SDN/2016/sdn1607info.htm and *Österreichische Akademie der Wissenschaften,* European Demographic Data Sheet 2018, https://www.oeaw.ac.at/fileadmin/NEWS/2018/PDF/VID_DataSheet2018_ Booklet_3.pdf.

19 See for instance the debate on "benefit tourism" in Germany: *Kersting*, Sozialtourismus, in: Bergmann, Handlexikon der Europäischen Union, 5th ed. 2015.

20 *Kochenov*, Brexit and the Argentinisation of British citizenship: Taking care not to overstay your 90 days in Rome, Amsterdam or Paris, VerfBlog, 24 June 2016, https://verfassungsblog.de/brexit-and-the-argentinisation-of-british-citizenship-taking-care-not-to-overstay-your-90-days-in-rome-amsterdam-or-paris/, DOI: http://dx.doi.org/10.17176/ 20160624-131913.

for Union and UK citizens, to enable the effective exercise of rights derived from Union law and based on past life choices, where those citizens have exercised free movement rights by the specified date."[21] Nonetheless, this agreement is still under the condition that a WA will be concluded. In the negative case, this principal mutual commitment on citizens' rights would be negatively affected by the caveat of the JR "*that nothing is agreed until everything is agreed*".[22] However, in November 2018 it still is unclear whether there will be a WA covering free movement of persons as had been sketched by the JR in December 2017 and specified by the European Commission in March 2018. Given the difficulties in the Brexit negotiations one may deplore the unpredictability and insecurity for all the EU/UK citizens who have relied on these rights. Consequently, it has been noted that an increasing number of citizens apply for additional citizenships, either of EU Member States or of the UK.

Accordingly, the following passage will refer to the intended UK rules for foreigners and briefly lay down the potential consequences and implications for EU citizens in the UK (1.).[23] Hereafter, the analysis will turn to the corresponding documents presented by the EU and the UK regarding the rights of citizens on free movement (2.). Finally, some general remarks will address the impact that Brexit might have on the concept of EU citizenship (3.).

1.   Free Movement of EU citizens after a "no-deal Brexit"

In the tensed atmosphere of Brexit negotiations, negotiators on both sides defend relatively strictly and inflexibly the corresponding positions regarding the modalities for a WA. Given that the aspect of limiting immigration was one of the main aspects that had influenced the outcome of the referendum in 2016, Brexiteers strive for excluding far-reaching rights for EU citizens.

---

21   Joint report from the negotiators of the European Union and the United Kingdom Government on progress during phase 1 of negotiations under Article 50 TEU on the United Kingdom's orderly withdrawal from the European Union, TF50 (2017) 19 – Commission to EU27, 8 December 2017.

22   *Ibid.*, Remarks.

23   With regard to these intended rules, the article will not repeat aspects that had been previously discussed elsewhere, see e.g.: *Mindus,* European Citizenship after Brexit, Freedom of Movement and Rights of Residence, 2017, or *Rathke,* Brexit und die Arbeitnehmerfreizügigkeit, in: *Kramme/Baldus/Schmidt-Kessel (eds.),* Brexit und die juristischen Folgen, 2016, pp. 211-229.

EU negotiators, however, emphasise the indivisibility of EU law – also with regard to the potential precedence of lax negotiations for other Member States that later might try to negotiate benefits. Accordingly, when the UK's international trade secretary Liam Fox stated that he saw a "60-40" chance of a no-deal Brexit,[24] the public was rather surprised by his bluntness and the extent of his pessimism, than about the realistic possibility that parties might fail to reach an agreement.

Currently, the EU citizens' rights to reside in the UK are exclusively governed by EU law which provides them a *permanent resident* status.[25] Hence, in the absence of a WA, EU citizens would depend on the rights granted under UK law. Given that the existing rules deal with the rights of third country nationals, the provisions do not precisely fit to the situation of EU citizens. Meanwhile, the UK government has published a "EU Settlement Scheme: Letter of Intent"[26] which provides some predictability for EU citizens living in the UK.[27]

---

24   *Hervey*, Liam Fox sees '60-40' chance of no-deal Brexit, 5 August, updated 6 August 2018, https://www.politico.eu/article/uk-trade-secretary-liam-fox-sees-60-40-chance-of-no-deal-brexit/.

25   Art. 16 ff. Directive 2004/38/EC of the European Parliament and of the Council of 29 April 2004 on the right of citizens of the Union and their family members to move and reside freely within the territory of the Member States, OJ 2004 L158/77.

26   *UK Home Office*, EU Settlement Scheme: Statement of Intent, 21 June 2018, https://assets.publishing.service.gov.uk/government/uploads/system/uploads/attachment_data/file/718237/EU_Settle-ment_Scheme_SOI_June_2018.pdf#page=6.

27   The following sources provide similar information: In its *White Paper* (full title: The United Kingdom's exit from and new partnership with the European Union White Paper, 2 February, updated 15 May 2017) the UK underlines its commitment to securing the rights of EU citizens residing in the UK, see point 6, https://www.gov.uk/government/publications/the-united-kingdoms-exit-from-and-new-partnership-with-the-european-union-white-paper. The *Policy Paper* The future relationship between the United Kingdom and the European Union published on 12 July 2018 by the Department for Exiting the European Union, confirms these statements in principle, https://www.gov.uk/government/publications/the-future-relationship-between-the-united-kingdom-and-the-european-union/the-future-relationship-between-the-united-kingdom-and-the-european-union-html-version#a-practical-brexit.

a)   The scheme as presented by the UK Government

According to these announcements,[28] to continue living in the UK after June 2021, EU citizens and their family members would need to apply for *settled status* – which under the *EU Settlement Scheme* means the right to continue to live and work in the UK after 31 December 2020. [29] After this scheme, EU citizens would be required to have started living in the UK before 1 January 2021 and have to apply to the scheme when it opens, even if they hold a registration certificate or permanent residence document.[30]

After getting *settled status*, EU citizens were entitled to stay in the UK indefinitely and to apply for British citizenship.[31] As the website indicates, EU citizens should be able to spend up to five years in a row outside the UK without losing their *settled status*. However, the definite answer how long they may live outside the UK is still subject to approval by Parliament.

Children born in the UK by EU citizens with *settled status* will automatically be British citizens.

The so-called *pre-settled status* (limited leave to remain for five years) would entitle the holder to stay in the UK for a further five years from the date after obtaining this status. Hereafter, as soon as having lived in the UK for five years and spent at least six months of each year in the UK, they may apply for *settled status* (indefinite leave to remain). According to the information published, EU citizens holding the pre-settled status should be able to spend up to two years in a row outside the UK without losing their *pre-*

---

28   The following information is based on the official statements by the UK Government on its website, titled: "Existing UK residence documents for EU citizens", https://www.gov.uk/uk-residence-eu-citizens .

29   https://www.gov.uk/settled-status-eu-citizens-families and the corresponding publication of the *UK Home Office*, EU Settlement Scheme: Statement of Intent, see note 26.

30   Ibid. at 1.6., pp. 5 ff.; Article 14 (16) and 17 Draft WA; Department for Exiting the European Union, "Legislating for the Withdrawal Agreement between the UK and the EU", 21 June 2018, pp 9, para 25, https://www.gov.uk/government/uploads/system/uploads/attachment_data/file/728757/6.4737_Cm9674 _Legislating_for_the_withdrawl_agree-ment_FINAL_230718_v3a_WEB _PM.pdf; *Guild*, Brexit and the Treatment of EU Citizens by the UK Home Office, CEPS Policy Insights, No 2017-33/September 2017, p. 3; available at https://ssrn.com/ab-stract=3053812.

31   The UK Government provides an overview of the main requirements at https://www.gov.uk/british-citizenship.

settled status. How long they may live outside the UK is still subject to approval by Parliament.

Both – the *settled* or *pre-settled status* – would provide the right to work in the UK, have access to the NHS, enrol in education or continue studying, to access public funds such as benefits and pensions (if eligible for them).

b)   Potential benefits and shortcomings of the UK scheme

At first glance, the announcements may reassure concerned EU citizens living in the UK. However, so far, the announcements only inform about the future prospect to apply for the corresponding status and do not indicate that EU citizens will have a right to obtain the status. Furthermore, the application procedure is not yet set up. According to publications regarding the current application process, it appears that factually, a considerable number of applicants does not succeed in the process.[32] Furthermore, it is deplored that UK institutions would exacerbate the application process in order to lower the number of migrants.[33]

Moreover, despite the overall relatively positive message to the EU citizens currently residing in the UK, important questions remain unsolved. For instance, aspects of social security, particularly regarding the coordination of contributions made to the national pension systems are not reflected by UK law, given that these aspects had previously been governed by EU secondary law, particularly regarding the coordination of social security ((EC) 883/2004). While the founding Member States may still have existing bilateral agreements with the UK on certain issues – as for instance Germany with an agreement concluded in 1960[34] – the EU8 Member States do not have corresponding agreements.

2.   Free Movement of persons under the draft WA

On 8 December 2017, the EU and the UK had in principal agreed on a range of important issues laid down in the Joint Report[35]. Regarding the overall

---

32   *Guild,* (note 30), p. 3
33   *Ibid.*
34   Abkommen vom 20. April 1960 zwischen der Bundesrepublik Deutschland und dem Vereinigten Königreich Großbritannien und Nordirland über Soziale Sicherheit, BGBl. 1961 II S. 241.
35   See note 21.

objective of a withdrawal agreement (WA) to be concluded, they agreed *"to provide reciprocal protection for Union and UK citizens, to enable the effective exercise of rights derived from Union law and based on past life choices, where those citizens have exercised free movement rights by the specified date."* The UK government, however, was divided on principal questions and thus did not propose further details. This explains why, on 28 February 2018, only the European Commission had published a more thorough draft for a WA which has become the basis of current negotiations.[36] This 168 Articles-comprehensive draft also addresses in several provisions the relevant issues for EU and UK citizens, i.e. regarding the rights related to residence, exit and entry as well as the rights for workers and self-employed persons. Furthermore, Title III deals with the coordination of social security systems. A later version of this document published on the website of the UK government visualizes the aspects both parties have agreed upon, respectively, where negotiations are still necessary and to what extent.[37] Regarding the rights on free movement of persons, both parties completely agree. Before commenting on these provisions, it should be noted that Art. 4 (1) para. 2 stipulates the following:

> "In particular, Union citizens and United Kingdom nationals shall be able to rely directly on the provisions contained or referred to in Part Two. Any provisions inconsistent or incompatible with that Part shall be disapplied."

Accordingly, citizens may directly rely on the provisions dealing specifically with the rights of citizens or workers on residence. Regarding the respective provisions, the draft WA generally aims at reflecting the overall objective of the JR. Most of these provisions aim at preserving the rights that UK and EU

---

36   *European Commission,* European Commission Draft Withdrawal Agreement on the withdrawal of the United Kingdom, TF50 (2018) 33 – Commission to EU27, 28 February 2018.

37   The *UK government* published a modified version on its website which contains marks on agreed passages: *UK government,* Draft Agreement on the withdrawal of the United Kingdom of Great Britain and Northern Ireland from the European Union and the European Atomic Energy Community, 19 March 2018, https://www.gov.uk/government/publications/draft-withdrawal-agreement-19-march-2018.

citizens currently enjoy,[38] even though at some instances the draft WA would decrease rights.[39]

The first part[40] is dedicated to Common Provisions, e.g. objectives, definitions, territorial scope and methods and principles. Part two draft WA deals with citizens' rights and, after defining central terms such as e.g. "family members", "frontier workers"[41] and the personal scope[42], Art. 10 draft WA clarifies that continuity of residency generally[43] shall not be affected by absences. Art. 11 draft WA stipulates that discrimination of persons comprised by the draft WA on the grounds of nationality shall be prohibited, referring to Art. 18 (subpara. 1) TFEU.

Chapter 1 (Art. 12-21 WA) lays down the rights to residence[44] as well as rules and conditions for the application process,[45] restrictions and safeguards.[46] These provisions largely maintain existing rights of EU citizens residing in the UK. For citizens from the EU who have decided to permanently reside in the UK, Art. 14 (1) 1st sentence draft WA is of particular relevance. The provision stipulates that:

> "Union citizens, United Kingdom nationals, and their respective family members, who have resided legally in accordance with Union law for a continuous period of five years in the host State, or for the duration specified in Article 17 of Directive 2004/38/EC, shall have the right to reside permanently in the host State under the conditions set out in Articles 16, 17 and 18 of Directive 2004/38/EC."

As indicated, other provisions of this chapter provide important clarifications. Already Art. 12 draft WA provides that EU/UK citizens shall have the right to reside in the host State while, by referring to EU law provisions, the

---

38 *Markakis*, Brexit Issues and Regulatory Approaches with Regard to Free Movement of Persons (17 July 2018), provides a comprehensive insight in the effect of the WA, p. 14, https://ssrn.com/abstract=3260542; also in print, forthcoming, *Kainer/Repasi* (eds.), Trade Relations after Brexit, 2019.

39 *Ibid.*, pp. 18 ff.

40 Art. 1-7 draft WA.

41 Art. 8 a) and b) draft WA.

42 Art. 9 draft WA.

43 Subject to Art. 14 (2) draft WA – which refers to Art. 16 (3) and Art. 21 Directive 2004/38/EC – and Art. 14 (3) draft WA stating that only a period of absence of more than five consecutive years affects the right of permanent residency.

44 Art. 12-16 draft WA.

45 Art. 17 draft WA.

46 Art. 18 and 19 draft WA.

norm specifies limitations and conditions. One potentially important difference to the currently applicable EU law is that the draft WA does not explicitly refer to Art. 20 TFEU. This might become relevant for constellations involving family members from third countries. Given that citizens from the EU8 are in the focus of this article, this aspect[47] will not be further discussed here.[48]

Art. 22 draft WA as the first provision of Chapter 2 governs the rights of workers, mostly by referring to provisions governing free movement of workers under Art. 45 TFEU[49]. In a similar way, Art. 23 draft WA lays down the rights for self-employed persons, referring to Art. 49 TFEU and to Art. 22 WA. Furthermore, Art. 25-27 draft WA determine the modalities for recognition of professional qualifications which globally follows the previous EU practice.

Title III (Art. 28 and 29 WA) deals with the coordination of social security systems. Referring to corresponding rules of EU law[50] this is thus one of the most striking aspects of relevance for EU citizens residing in the UK that would considerably go beyond the above-mentioned rules envisaged by the UK.[51]

Overall, the provisions laid down in the draft WA regarding residence rights largely correspond to the existing rights under EU law. Accordingly, it appears that citizens residing in the UK/EU will enjoy similar rights to

---

47 This aspect is mostly relevant for third country nationals who may be family members of EU citizens; for more extensive explanation see *Markakis*, (note 38), p. 13. Also regarding a potential problem of UK citizens who may remain *landlocked* in the EU Member States of residence, *ibid.*

48 *Department for Exiting the European Union*, "Legislating for the Withdrawal Agreement between the UK and the EU", 21 June 2018, clarifies the scope of the term *family member*, explicitly referring to ECJ case law, at 6.7-6.12, pp. 27-30, https://www.gov.uk/government/uploads/system/uploads/attachment_data/file/728757/6.4737_Cm9674_Legislating_for_the_withdrawl_agreement_FINAL_230718_v3a_WEB_PM.pdf.

49 Furthermore, Art. 22 (1) draft WA refers to Regulation No. 492/211 of the European Parliament and of the Council of 5 April 2011 on freedom of movement for workers within the Union, OJ 2011 L 141/1.

50 Art. 28 and 29 draft WA in various instances refer to Regulation No 883/2004 of the European Parliament and of the Council of 29 April 2004 on the coordination of social security systems, OJ 2004 L 166/1.

51 *Department for Exiting the European Union*, "Legislating for the Withdrawal Agreement between the UK and the EU", note 48, p 18, para. 41 provides some further explanations on these provisions.

reside in the UK as they do today. Furthermore, given that the draft WA comprises rules on the coordination of social security systems that widely correspond to the existing practice, the WA would facilitate life for these persons compared to a *no-deal Brexit* scenario as presented above.

3.   Brexit and EU Citizenship

Regarding either of the previously described scenarios it appears that the most important rights of EU/UK citizens currently residing in the UK, respectively in the EU, will be upheld.

Apart from the relevance for citizens, the questions regarding the effect of Brexit on rights granted under EU citizenship are of high importance for the concept of EU citizenship in the future. Differently to the market freedoms – which are intrinsically linked to the market, where workers as economic actors to a certain degree may always be affected by the changing economic policies of their national states, respectively of their trade partners – EU citizenship also has a different political and ideological basis and, hence, partially follows different aims. Its' concept fundamentally differs in that regard, as it is intended to establish a bond existing beyond the market and – by attributing EU citizens a *fundamental status*[52] – is directly addressed to the citizens, not to the economic actor. The perspective of an unordered Brexit with the consequence of Art. 50 (3) TEU that "[…] the Treaties cease to apply […]"would jeopardize this concept.

Having been created under the Treaty of Maastricht in 1993 with the rather minimalistic provision *in Art. 20 TFEU*, EU citizenship has considerably evolved over the past decades. Years after AG Jacobs had presented his visionary concept to entitle EU the citizen to "[…] say 'civis europeus sum' and to invoke that status in order to oppose any violation of his fundamental rights", the ECJ gradually adopted this approach, developing EU citizenship as a "fundamental status".[53] Today, even though Art. 20 (1) TFEU closely links the concept to the citizenship of an EU Member State, it provides EU

---

52   ECJ, *Grzelczyk*, Case C-184/99, [2001] ECR I-6193, para. 31.
53   It suffices to mention some decisions such as ECJ, *Grzelczyk*, Case C-184/99, [2001] ECR I-6193, para. 31; ECJ, *Zhu and Chen*, Case C-200/02, [2004] ECR I-9925, para 25; or *Zambrano*, Case C-34/09, [2011] ECR I-1177, para 41.

citizens with considerable rights of EU-wide dimension.[54] As a consequence, regarding the growing number of EU citizens residing in other Member States,[55] they rely on EU law and increasingly seem to trust in the persistence and validity of their rights to free movement. Furthermore, in 2018 respondents communicated in an Eurobarometer poll that they felt as EU citizens.[56]

An unordered Brexit, depriving EU/UK citizens of all corresponding rights against their will,[57] from the moment of the withdrawal from the EU on, would mean a severe setback to this concept. The failure to secure this carefully elaborated and previously highly praised *fundamental status* would imply that the concept lacked credibility and sustainability and thus expose it as a hollow ideology. This message, however, would not only concern the citizens who lose these rights but, moreover, affect the entire concept in the future of the EU27.

This aspect is not to be confused with the deplorable reality that, as a consequence of a democratic decision in the Brexit-referendum, the British people had voted for the loss of the corresponding rights.[58] The argument rather underlines the fragile character of EU citizenship if it failed to preserve any of the rights it previously comprised, (only) due to the withdrawal of a Member State. This aspect goes beyond the current Brexit debate, given that the same question is raised in the context of potential secessions of EU Member

---

54   This still holds true despite a more restrictive tendency in the more recent CJEU case law as extensively shown by *Haltern*, Europarecht, Band II, 2017, p. 899, para. 2069 ff.

55   Eurostat news release, 87/2018 – 28 May 2018, EU citizens in other EU Member States,   p.   3,   https://ec.europa.eu/eurostat/documents/2995521/8926076/3-28052018-AP-EN.pdf/48c473e8-c2c1-4942-b2a4-5761edacda37.

56   European Commission, Standard Eurobarometer No. 89 (Spring 2018), p. 31, ec.europa.eu/commfrontoffice/publicopinion/index.cfm/ResultDoc/download/DocumentKy/83538.

57   This aspect is a fundamental difference to the situation of the case *Rottmann* (ECJ, Case C-135/08, [2010] ECR I-1449) where the loss of EU citizenship resulted from the citizens' own acting.

58   *Kochenov*, EU Citizenship and Withdrawals from the Union: How Inevitable Is the Radical Downgrading of Rights?, 2016; *ibid.*, Misguided 'Associate EU Citizenship' Talk as a Denial of EU Values, VerfBlog, 1 March 2018, https://verfassungsblog.de/misguided-associate-eu-citizenship-talk-as-a-denial-of-eu-values/, DOI: https://dx.doi.org/10.17176/20180301-134525, points out that *Verhofstatt* ignored this aspect when advocating in favour of an Associate EU citizenship.

States and the fate of their citizens.[59] However, in the context of Brexit it currently appears that proposals for *associated EU citizenship*[60] will not become necessary – neither for EU/UK citizens nor for saving the legal concept.

C.   Conclusion

The referendum in the UK to leave the EU came as a shock for EU citizens who had decided to permanently work and live in the UK. With more than a third of the EU citizens residing in the UK originating from the EU8, Brexit at first sight appears to have an increased significance for them. However, with regard to the continuing negotiations of the WA, all EU/UK citizens residing abroad are equally concerned and all desire predictability and legal certainty.

In order to secure the rights of these citizens, the draft for a WA elaborated by the European Commission dedicates a chapter to these aspects. In March 2018, the UK government responded positively to this draft WA and, in addition, has published a statement of intent regarding the EU settlement scheme in case that the negotiations on other aspects of the WA fail. In this statement the UK government clarifies that it widely intends to grant similar rights to those suggested by the European Commission. As a result, notwithstanding the success of the negotiations for a WA, it appears that EU citizens who work and reside in the UK will maintain their current rights of residence. Differently, however, the specific rights regarding social coordination would not be covered in the case of a *no deal* Brexit and thus to a high degree depend on the success of the ongoing negotiations of the WA.

Apart from the relief for EU/UK citizens, these overall (relatively) positive prospects are also a positive sign for the concept of EU citizenship. An unordered Brexit, depriving EU/UK citizens of all corresponding rights even against their will, would considerably affect the credibility of this concept.

---

59   However, the concept is not yet solved, given that similar challenges may arise in other constellations as for instance in potential separations from EU such as Catalunya where Catalan citizens might immediately be stripped of their EU citizenship whether they would have opted for Catalan independence or not. *Fassbender*, Die EU besteht ihre Probe nicht, FAZ, 27.10.2017, http://www.faz.net/aktuell/politik/ausland/katalonien-krise-wird-die-eu-ihrer-rolle-gerecht-15263281.html.

60   *Roeben*, The Feasibility of Associate EU Citizenship for UK Citizens Post-Brexit (14 May 2018). Available at https://ssrn.com/abstract=3178055 or http://dx.doi.org/10.2139/ssrn.3178055.

The reliability and substance of a concept, supposed to grant citizens a "fundamental status", would have been shattered if it entirely failed to protect them from the moment of Brexit.

The Future Relationship between EU and UK – "Bilateral Agreements" EU – Switzerland as a Model?

Astrid Epiney and Sian Affolter

A.   Introduction

In the wake of the forthcoming withdrawal of the United Kingdom from the European Union, the question arises as to the form of the relations between the (future) third country United Kingdom and the EU. One possible scenario would be that these relations were to be regulated in one or more agreement(s) between the UK and the EU. At present, only the very vague outlines of possible objectives – which would have to be agreed upon by both parties – of such agreements, have become apparent. It remains unanswered if and if yes to what extent the UK seeks to continue to participate in the internal market or parts of it or whether it rather seeks to conclude a "simple" free trade agreement. For several different levels of cooperation, the latter solution would, however, provide for.

The first version – which would, in the end, result in a type of soft Brexit – gives rise to complex questions. It would essentially imply that the respect of certain EU law requirements would furthermore need to be ensured, which, in turn, relates to the issues of the updating of agreements and dispute settlement. In the framework of the latter, clarification of the role of the Court of Justice of the European Union (ECJ) is needed.

Such close interlocking with or a genuine participation in the internal market or parts of it of third states can already be observed in two cases: On the one hand, in the framework of the European Economic Area (EEA) and, on the other hand, in the case of the Bilateral Agreements between the EU and Switzerland. Since an accession of the UK to the EEA currently appears unlikely, the question arises as to whether the Bilateral Agreements Switzerland–EU could provide for a type of model for the design of the relations between the UK and the Union. The present contribution aims to present the Bilateral Agreements Switzerland–EU against this background: After an overview of the material scope of the agreements (B.), the characteristics of the latter shall be outlined (C.), before discussing the so called institutional questions which have been in the centre of attention these last years (D.), and presenting, in a synthesis, the probable characteristics a "Swiss model" would entail (E.). In the form of an excursus (F.), the issue of the relations between the UK and third countries (such as Switzerland) shall be addressed before rounding off the contribution with a short conclusion (G.)

B.   The Bilaterales: Scope

The so-called "bilateral way" was developed following the negative vote on 6 December 1992 as to the question whether Switzerland should join the EEA.[1] The main underlying idea was (or still is) to develop closer ties with the internal market, as this is regarded as being essential, for Switzerland. Furthermore, a certain number of further, specific questions were integrated in the approach because the European Union and/or Switzerland were (and still are) interested in international agreements in these matters.

Thus, two packages of "Bilateral Agreements" were concluded in 1999 and in 2004, covering various areas and containing mechanisms, which integrate EU law into the agreements to ensure compatibility between the legal situation in the European Union and Switzerland in the respective areas.[2]

The first package of 1999 comprises seven agreements concerning the following domains:[3]

- mutual recognition in relation to conformity assessment (technical barriers to trade);
- trade in agricultural products;
- scientific and technological cooperation (research);

---

[1] The following chapter is largely based on research conducted in another context, see in particular *Epiney/Affolter*, The Swiss Way: 120 Agreements but no Perspective?, in: Giegerich/Schmitt/Zeitzmann (eds.), Flexibility in the EU and Beyond: How Much Differentiation Can European Integration Bear?, 2017, p. 197 f.

[2] See for more details on the agreements *Epiney/Metz/Pirker*, Zur Parallelität der Rechtsentwicklung in der EU und in der Schweiz: Ein Beitrag zur rechtlichen Tragweite der "Bilateralen Abkommen", 2012, p. 95 f.; *Oesch*, Switzerland and the European Union: General Framework, Bilateral Agreements, Autonomous Adaptation, 2018, p. 19 f.; *Cottier* et al., Die Rechtsbeziehungen der Schweiz und der Europäischen Union, 2014, p. 79 f.; for an overview, see *Pirker/Epiney*, The Integration of Switzerland into the Framework of EU Law by Means of the "Bilateral Agreements", in: Müller-Graff/Mestad (eds.), The Rising Complexity of European Law, 2014, p. 39 (40 f.).

[3] See Decision of the Council and of the Commission 2002/309/EC about the Agreement on Scientific and Technological Cooperation, of 4 April 2002 on the conclusion of seven Agreements with the Swiss Confederation, OJ 2002 L 114, p. 1.

- public procurement;
- air transport;
- land transport;
- free movement of persons.

The second package of 2004 contains agreements on the following topics:[4]
- processed agricultural products;[5]
- participation of Switzerland in the European Environmental Agency and the European Environment Information and Observation Network;[6]
- statistics;[7]
- media;[8]
- youth and professional education;

---

4   See Botschaft zur Genehmigung der bilateralen Abkommen zwischen der Schweiz und der Europäischen Union, einschliesslich der Erlasse zur Umsetzung der Abkommen ("Bilaterale II"), of 1 October 2004; for the text of the agreements see BBl Bundesblatt (Federal Gazette of the Swiss federal government), 2004, p. 5965.

5   See Agreement between the European Community and the Swiss Confederation amending the Agreement between the European Economic Community and the Swiss Confederation of 22 July 1972 as regards the provisions applicable to processed agricultural products, attached to Council Decision 2005/45/EC of 22 December 2004 concerning the conclusion and the provisional application of the Agreement between the European Community and the Swiss Confederation amending the Agreement between the European Economic Community and the Swiss Confederation of 22 July 1972 as regards the provisions applicable to processed agricultural products, OJ 2005 L 23, p. 17.

6   See Council Decision of 27 February 2006 on the conclusion, on behalf of the European Community, of the Agreement between the European Community and the Swiss Confederation concerning the latter's participation in the European Environment Agency and the European Environment Information and Observation Network, OJ 2006 L 90, p. 36.

7   See Agreement between the European Community and the Swiss Confederation on cooperation in the field of statistics, attached to Council Decision of 27 February 2006 on the conclusion of the Agreement between the European Community and the Swiss Confederation on cooperation in the field of statistics, OJ 2006 L 90, p. 1.

8   See Agreement between the European Community and the Swiss Confederation in the audio-visual field, establishing the terms and conditions for the participation of the Swiss Confederation in the Community programme MEDIA 2007, attached to Council Decision of 28 September 2007 concerning the signature and provisional application of an Agreement between the European Community and the Swiss Confederation in the audio-visual field, establishing the terms and conditions for the participation of the Swiss Confederation in the Community programme MEDIA 2007, and a Final Act, OJ 2007 L 303, p. 9.

- fraud combat;[9]
- taxation of savings income;[10]
- Schengen and Dublin;[11]
- pensions.

Apart from these agreements contained in the so-called "Bilateral Agreements I and II", many other important agreements between the European Union (and sometimes also its Member States) and Switzerland exist, with some of them having been concluded before the mentioned Bilateral Agreements and others after the conclusion of the second package. For example, the Free Trade Agreement from 1972[12] is still of high importance and in 2009, a new

---

9   See Cooperation agreement between the European Community and its Member States, of the one part, and the Swiss Confederation, of the other part, to combat fraud and any other illegal activity to the detriment of their financial interests, attached to Council Decision of 18 December 2008 concerning the signature, on behalf of the European Community, of the Cooperation Agreement between the European Community and its Member States, of the one part, and the Swiss Confederation, of the other part, to combat fraud and any other illegal activity to the detriment of their financial interests, OJ 2009 L 46, p. 6.

10 See Agreement between the European Community and the Swiss Confederation providing for measures equivalent to those laid down in Council Directive 2003/48/EC on taxation of savings income in the form of interest payments, attached to Council Decision 2004/911/EC of 2 June 2004 on the signing and conclusion of the Agreement between the European Community and the Swiss Confederation providing for measures equivalent to those laid down in Council Directive 2003/48/EC on taxation of savings income in the form of interest payments and the accompanying Memorandum of Understanding, OJ 2004 L 385, p. 28.

11 See Agreement between the European Community and the Swiss Confederation concerning the criteria and mechanisms for establishing the State responsible for examining a request for asylum lodged in a Member State or in Switzerland, attached to Council Decision 2008/147/EC of 28 January 2008 on the conclusion on behalf of the European Community of the Agreement between the European Community and the Swiss Confederation concerning the criteria and mechanisms for establishing the State responsible for examining a request for asylum lodged in a Member State or in Switzerland, OJ L 53, p. 5, and Agreement between the European Union, the European Community and the Swiss Confederation on the Swiss Confederation's association with the implementation, application and development of the Schengen *acquis*, attached to Council Decision 2008/149/JHA of 28 January 2008 on the conclusion on behalf of the European Union of the Agreement between the European Union, the European Community and the Swiss Confederation on the Swiss Confederation's association with the implementation, application and development of the Schengen *acquis*, OJ 2008 L 53, p. 50.

12 See Accord entre la Communauté économique européenne et la Confédération suisse, attached to Règlement (CEE) no. 2840/72 du Conseil, du 19 décembre 1972, portant conclusion d'un accord entre la Communauté économique européenne et la Confédération suisse, arrêtant des dispositions pour son application

Agreement on Customs Security Measures[13] entered into force. Overall, about 120 agreements on various topics exist and there are probably only very few who truly know all these agreements in detail.

Furthermore, the European Union and Switzerland plan to conclude further agreements in a certain number of areas. Currently negotiations are ongoing regarding an agreement on electricity and an agreement on agriculture, food safety, product safety and public health.[14] However, the conclusion of these agreements is, now, dependent on whether a solution to the problem of the so-called "institutional matters"[15] is found or, in other words, whether the parties manage to conclude a so-called "institutional framework agreement". This is due to the Union's persistent stance that there will be no future agreements granting access to the internal market if the institutional matters have not been resolved. [16]

Many and the most important agreements of the so called "Bilaterales" foresee the integration of Switzerland into parts of the internal market respectively the EU *acquis*, which causes for several complex and open questions. Central to and signifying for the discussion is the tension between bedding such agreements into the framework of classic international public law, on the one hand, with them at the same time aiming at allowing a third state to participate in the EU internal market which involves the agreements "taking over" supranational EU law, on the other hand.

---

et portant conclusion de l'accord additionnel sur la validité pour la principauté de Liechtenstein de l'accord entre la Communauté économique européenne et la Confédération suisse du 22 juillet 1972, OJ 1972 L 300, p. 189.

13   See Agreement between the European Community and the Swiss Confederation on the simplification of inspections and formalities in respect of the carriage of goods and on customs security measures, attached to Council Decision 2009/556/EC of 25 June 2009 concerning the provisional application and conclusion of the Agreement between the European Community and the Swiss Confederation on the simplification of inspections and formalities in respect of the carriage of goods and on customs security measures, OJ 2009 L 199, p. 24.

14   For an overview on current developments see the website of the Swiss Directorate for European Affairs (DEA) https://www.eda.admin.ch/dea/en/home/verhandlungen-offene-themen/verhandlungen.html (last accessed on 24 September 2018).

15   Cf. below chapter IV.

16   See, e.g., the Council conclusions on EU relations with the Swiss Confederation of 28 February 2017, Press Release 93/17.

C.   The *Bilaterales*: Characteristics

I.   Overview

The Bilateral Agreements present several common features, which, however, can differ between the Bilateral Agreements I and the Bilateral Agreements II. Certain agreements can also present very specific features.[17] In general,[18] the Bilateral Agreements constitute classical international and thus not actual integration agreements in the sense of a genuine integration of Switzerland into the EU. This general approach can be seen, on the one hand, in the content of the agreements (which are based on the principle of the equivalence of legislation or of standards and do not foresee an actual integration into the EU *acquis*) and, on the other hand, in the institutional structure which corresponds to the "classic structure of international public law".

In the following, a presentation of the characteristics of the Bilateral Agreements cannot be extensively.[19] Indeed, it is rather only the most central aspects, which shall be illustrated.

-   The agreements contained in the two packages of the Bilateral Agreements each constitute separate, self-contained treaties. At present, there is no overarching framework agreement regulating cross-

---

17   The following chapter is largely based on research conducted in another context, see in particular *Epiney/Metz/Pirker* (note 2); *Epiney/Affolter* (note 1); see furthermore *Epiney*, Zur institutionellen Struktur der Bilateralen Abkommen – Bestandsaufnahme, Perspektiven und Bewertung, in: Keller/Wiprächtiger (eds.), FS Amstutz, Recht zwischen Dogmatik und Theorie, 2012, p. 35 f.; *Epiney*, Beziehungen Schweiz-EU: status quo und Perspektiven, in: Schellenbauer/Schwarz (eds.), Bilateralismus – was sonst? Eigenständigkeit trotz Abhängigkeit, 2015, p. 25 f., each with further references.

18   An exception can be seen in the Agreement on Air Transport which forms part of the Bilateral Agreements I. This agreement foresees a genuine integration into the EU *acquis*, in particular regarding the competences of the Union's institutions (cf. Art. 20 of the agreement). Furthermore, The Schengen and Dublin Association Agreements can be seen as agreements resulting in partial integration, when taking into account Switzerland's rather extensive obligations with regard to "taking over" the relevant parts of the EU *acquis* and its development, as it will be discussed further below.

19   Cf. in this regard *Jaag/Zihlmann*, Institutionen und Verfahren, in: Thürer et al., Bilaterale Verträge I & II, 2007, p. 65 f.; *Felder*, Cadre institutionnel et dispositions générales des accords bilatéraux II (sauf Schengen/Dublin), in: Kaddous/Greiner (eds.), Accords bilatéraux II Suisse – UE et autres accords récents, p. 93 f.

sectoral issues or questions. Such an agreement is, however, currently being negotiated regarding the institutional questions, as will be shown below.

- Despite constituting separate agreements, there are certain links or connections between the agreements. Regarding the Bilateral Agreements II, the connection is solely of political nature. Regarding the Bilateral Agreements I, however, the connection is of a legal nature. The seven agreements constitute a package insofar as that the final provisions of each agreement foresee that they can only enter into force together and that the non-renewal or termination of one agreement would lead to the other agreements also no longer being applied.[20]

- The substantive content is, in principle, static. The often-foreseen possibility of further developing the agreements' content – in particular about updating the agreements' content in line with developments in EU law – does not change much in this regard, at least structurally, since the updating must be explicitly agreed to by both (or all) parties. Thus, the material scope of the agreements, in principle, corresponds to EU legislation in force at the point of signature of the agreements and an update due to new developments requires the consent of the treaty parties. This may take place in the so-called joint committee where applicable.

However, this does not change the fact that it is possible to establish a link to the EU *acquis*. This can be done by using various techniques. If this link is established by the inclusion of references to EU law into the agreement or its annexes, the agreements are generally based on the principle of the equivalency of legislation. According to this principle the inclusion of references does not entail an obligation to formally create an equal legal situation. It is rather regarding the content of the legislation applied, that the criterion of equivalency is pertinent. The Agreement on Air Transport and the Schengen and Dublin Association Agreements form an exception to this rule. Here, the EU legal acts referred to are to be implemented

---

20   See, e. g., Art. 25 para. 4 of the Agreement between the European Community and its Member States, of the one part, and the Swiss Confederation, of the other, on the free movement of persons (Agreement on the Free Movement of Persons) of 30 April 2002, OJ, L 114, p.6.

and applied in Switzerland,[21] thus making Switzerland "genuinely" bound by the relevant EU legal acts.

- Furthermore, the agreements only cover certain areas. Thus, a sectoral approach is followed and – unlike the EEA – it is not about ensuring full participation in the internal market, but rather only about partial participation (even if the agreements seen together assure a participation in essential parts of the internal market and some other areas of EU law).

- Regarding the content of the agreements, it can be differentiated between cooperation agreements, which focus on the cooperation of the treaty parties in certain areas or the participation of Switzerland in certain EU-programs, liberalisation- and harmonisation-agreements and, lastly, (partial) integration-agreements.

- The application and interpretation of the agreements lie, in principle, in the hands of the responsible authorities or courts of the treaty parties. This is in line with the fact that the agreements constitute treaties of classic public international law. Thus, it is up to the treaty parties to apply and interpret the agreements. However, several exceptions to this rule can be observed:

First, certain agreements oblige the treaty parties to create or name specific authorities or the agreement itself names the responsible authorities. This is the case, e.g., for the Agreement on the Environment with regard to setting up the network EIONET,[22] for the Agreement on the Taxation of Savings Income,[23] or for the Agreement on Public Procurement which contains an obligation to create a specific surveillance authority.[24] Therefore, the autonomy of the treaty parties with regard to the manner of implementation of the agreements is reduced. This is, however, only of organisational nature.

---

21 Cf. the wording in Art. 2 para. 2 of the Agreement concluded by the Council of the European Union and the Republic of Iceland and the Kingdom of Norway concerning the latters' association with the implementation, application and development of the Schengen acquis (Schengen Association Agreement) of 10 July 1999, OJ, L 176, p. 36.

22 Cf. Art. 5 Agreement on the Environment (note 6).

23 Art. 11 in connection with Annex I of the Agreement between the European Community and the Swiss Confederation providing for measures equivalent to those laid down in Council Directive 2003/48/EC on taxation of savings income in the form of interest payments (Agreement on the Taxation of Savings Income), of 29 December 2004, OJ, L 385, p.30.

24 Art. 8 Agreement on Public Procurement (note 3).

Second, the application of important parts of the Agreement on Air Transport is subject to the competent institutions at EU level, thus the Commission and the ECJ.[25] In this case, contrary to above, it is not only at an organisational level that the autonomy of the different treaty parties is restricted but it is rather about granting the EU's institutions legally substantive decision-making powers.

Finally, certain agreements – the Research and the MEDIA Agreement[26] – foresee that EU institutions can conduct financial controls in Switzerland. This is since the agreements ensure Switzerland's participation in EU-programs and thus the access to EU funds. Again, in this case substantive powers of decision or control are assigned to the EU, however, to a rather restricted extent.

- Since many agreements foresee mechanisms for updating the agreement's content in view of aligning with developments taking place at the level of EU legislation, regard must also be directed towards possible rights of participation of Switzerland in the legislative process of the EU, thus possible decision-shaping powers. The agreements often allow for a certain participation of Switzerland when legal acts, which will or may be included into the respective agreement are concerned. The relevant provisions or issued declarations towards Switzerland[27] foresee that Swiss representatives can participate in the role of observers in meetings of committees and expert groups of the council when legal acts or legislative projects are discussed which could be of importance for the development of the agreements. Furthermore, participation at actual council meetings is also possible. The design of this possibility is especially far-reaching in the context of the Schengen and Dublin Association. However, it is important to note that participation remains, also here, constricted to being granted advisory rights.

- Finally, examination of the institutional structure is needed. In general,[28] the agreements foresee a joint committee, which is constituted

---

25   Art. 11, 20 Agreement on Air Transport (note 3).
26   Annex C Agreement on Research, Annex IV MEDIA Agreement (note 3 and note 8).
27   In relation to the Bilateral Agreements I, these "rights" were enshrined in a declaration (Erklärung zur Teilnahme der Schweiz an den Ausschüssen, included in the final acts of the agreements), in the Bilateral Agreements II they can sometimes be found in the agreements themselves.
28   Exceptions in the sense of an agreement not foreseeing a joint committee can be seen in the Agreements on the Taxation of Savings Income and on Pensions as

by representatives of the European Union on the one hand and representatives of Switzerland, on the other hand. The competences of these joint committees generally extend to three important areas:

- The exchange of information, consultation and other "soft" mechanisms to ensure the functioning of the agreement;
- the settlement of disputes with, however, no possibility of taking decisions which are binding on the parties;
- and the taking of binding decisions as far as this is explicitly provided for in the agreement. In this regard, it is primarily the competences to update the references to secondary law contained in the annexes and to take decisions on protective measures, which are of importance.

In the following, We will look at two characteristics or rather institutional aspects in a more detailed manner. First, the question of the different mechanisms of integrating EU law into the agreements or of integrating Switzerland into the internal market will be discussed. Then, the contribution will go on to examine the question of the interpretation of the Bilateral Agreements in more detail.

II.   "Integration Mechanisms" in the Framework of the Bilateral Agreements

As mentioned above, the Bilateral Agreements cover a very large range of rather different topics. However, some of the most important among these, e.g. the Agreement on Free Movement of Persons, the Agreements on Air and Land Transport or the Agreements on the Schengen and Dublin *acquis*, aim for a "partial integration" of Switzerland into the EU *acquis*. In other words, they should guarantee that the relevant and defined EU *acquis* also applies to Switzerland, in a way that is parallel to a Member State. To reach this goal, different techniques have been outlined which are intended to ensure the "integration" of the relevant EU law into the bilateral agreements.

The present section first deals with the integration of the EU *acquis* now of conclusion of the agreements (1.), before turning the focus towards the mechanisms for developing the agreements in line with developments of EU law (2.).

---

well as in the Agreement on Education. The Agreement on Trade in Agricultural Products foresees two joint committees.

1.   Integration of the EU Acquis now of Conclusion

The Bilateral Agreements mainly operate through two different mechanisms when they intend to "include" or "integrate" parts of EU law into the framework of the agreements:

First, many articles of the agreements merely copy the wording of the relevant provisions of EU law, sometimes, however, with slight adaptations to the text (e.g. referring to contracting parties instead of Member States). For example, the Agreement on Public Procurement provides for a principle of non-discrimination on grounds of nationality in its Art. 6; this principle is also taken on in Art. 2 of the Agreement on the Free Movement of Persons. The latter agreement also transposes several free movement rights from the relevant EU primary and secondary law in its Annex I. In this context, the question may arise as to the extent to which the articles of the Bilateral Agreements really aim to integrate EU law and whether they are to be interpreted in the same way as EU law.

Many agreements also refer directly to EU secondary acts, usually in their annexes. Therefore, these annexes contain lists of secondary acts and the contracting parties are required to apply either EU secondary law or equivalent norms. In such cases, Switzerland is effectively bound to apply EU secondary law or at least to create an equivalent legal framework. Examples in this context are the Annexes II and III to the Agreement on the Free Movement of Persons (containing lists of secondary acts on mutual recognition of diplomas and social security) or the Annexes to the Schengen and Dublin Association Agreements, containing lists of the relevant EU *acquis*. This mechanism seems to be the EU's preferred system in the context of the Bilateral Agreements, since it ensures a (relatively) far-reaching adoption of the requirements of EU law also in the relations to Switzerland and facilitates the development of the agreement, as it will be shown in the following.

However, also the agreements integrating parts of the EU acquis contain "autonomous" articles, which do not refer to EU law. So, Art. 24 annexe I of the Agreement on the Free Movement of Persons foresees some special exceptions as the scope of the agreement is concerned.

2.   Development of the Agreements

The integration of EU law through the framework of the Bilateral Agreements is based on the state of EU law when the treaty is signed. In this respect, the Bilateral Agreements are static agreements and follow a "traditional" approach of international law. However, EU law is subject to constant change. Therefore, the aim of the agreements designed to achieve a certain level of integration, which is to guarantee a parallel between the legal situation in the European Union and in the relationship with Switzerland implies, in the fields covered by the agreements, the necessity of integrating new EU law developments into the framework of the agreements. Three mechanisms can be distinguished in this respect:

- First, the agreement may be revised. Such a revision is, of course, perfectly possible under international law; however, it involves a complicated procedure requiring new negotiations, signature and ratification of the contracting parties, requirements which are especially important with respect to the treaties also (jointly) concluded by the Member States (mixed agreements). It is, thus, not surprising that this mechanism is not very practicable, and the contracting parties have never used it in the context of the Bilateral Agreements to date.

- Second, agreements, which contain lists of EU secondary acts in their annexes generally foresee that the joint committee (composed of representatives of the contracting parties) can take the binding decision to modify and adapt the annexes which subsequently implies the possibility to carry over new EU legal developments into the framework of the agreement. Since the joint committees decide by unanimity, both contracting parties must agree on such an integration of new legal developments.

- Finally, some agreements, especially those concerning Schengen and Dublin, provide for a "de facto-obligation" of Switzerland to take over new legal developments in the fields covered by the agreements. Switzerland is free to apply its normal legislative procedure for this purpose, but the sanction for non-adaptation to the future Schengen or Dublin *acquis* consists of, in principle, termination of the whole agreement.[29] A less far-reaching system in this context is foreseen in the Agreement on Customs Security Measures. According to Art. 29 para. 1 of said agreement, a treaty party (de facto the EU) is entitled to take "appropriate rebalancing measures", which includes the suspension of the provisions of chapter III on customs security measures, if the "equivalence of the Contracting Parties' custom security measures is no longer assured" (thus or de facto if

---

29   See Art. 7 para. 4 Schengen Association Agreement.

Switzerland fails to take over developments of EU law in the relevant area). The joint committee of the agreement can then ask an arbitral tribunal to examine the proportionality of the measures taken.

The second and the third of the mechanisms can provide for a legal development of the agreements, which "follows" the relevant amendments of EU law. However, these mechanisms generally do not apply to the parts of the agreements, which replicate the wording of EU law. Thus, if the agreements apply the technique of taking over the wording only, the legal development of the agreements following amendments of EU law can only be realised by modifications using the "normal" procedures of international law which is – as mentioned – not very realistic. The consequence of this situation is that there are – especially as far as the first package of Bilateral Agreements is concerned – important parts of the agreements, which are based on the legal situation in the EU at the time of signature, even though EU law has, in the meantime, been amended. Therefore, the legal parallel (or the so-called homogeneity) which should have been attained is only partially realised. As an important example, one may refer to Annex I to the Agreement on Free Movement of Persons: this annex contains the different rights of free movement and has to a large extent copied the wording of the relevant directives (but also of some articles of the treaties) which have in the meantime been abolished and replaced by Directive 2004/38.[30] The joint committee cannot decide to integrate this directive into the agreement since the reference by listing the relevant secondary acts to EU but by replicating the wording of EU law. The joint committee does not, therefore, have the competence to modify Annex I to the Agreement in this respect.

With regard to the interest of the EU regarding the integration of developments at EU level in the relevant areas, it can be observed that the EU appears to prefer foreseeing a "de facto obligation" to carry over developments, as it can be seen in the Schengen Association Agreement.[31] With regard to the future development of the relationship between Switzerland and the EU, as

---

30   Directive 2004/38/EC of the European Parliament and of the Council of 29 April 2004 on the right of citizens of the Union and their family members to move and reside freely within the territory of the Member States amending Regulation (EEC) No 1612/68 and repealing Directives 64/221/EEC, 68/360/EEC, 72/194/EEC, 73/148/EEC, 75/34/EEC, 75/35/EEC, 90/364/EEC, 90/365/EEC and 93/96/EEC, OJ 2004 L 158, p. 77.

31   Cf. already NZZ of 9.12.2008, EU-Mitgliedstaaten äußern sich kritisch zur Schweiz.

it will be analysed below, it seems unlikely that Switzerland will manage to disregard this demand completely.

Finally, when talking about the integration of developments of the relevant EU *acquis*, it is to be pointed out that the question of whether a specific EU legal act constitutes a development of the *acquis* relevant to an agreement can sometimes appear to be a difficult one to answer. For example, the new General Data Protection Regulation[32] is not seen as a development relevant to the Schengen Association Agreement, even though the previous directive[33] (which has been repealed by the new regulation) was being part of the relevant *acquis*.[34]

III.   The Interpretation of the Bilateral Agreements

The Bilateral Agreements are international treaties in the sense of the Vienna Convention on the Law of Treaties[35] (VCLT) (this convention only applying directly to treaties between States but also containing a large part of, as far as the interpretation of treaties is concerned, customary international law). Thus, their interpretation has to follow the relevant principles of international law and the specific rules of interpretation in EU law cannot – as such – be applied to the Bilateral Agreements.[36] However, applying the principles of interpretation of international law may lead to those parts of Bilateral Agreements reproducing EU law having to be interpreted in the same way as those articles or secondary acts are interpreted in the framework of EU law, for example by taking into account the rulings of the ECJ ("parallel interpretation"): Art. 31 of the VCLT sets out a number of elements to be used when interpreting international treaties:

   –   First, with respect to the ordinary meaning, the use of the same wording as in EU law and/or the reference to EU secondary legislation

---

32   Regulation (EU) 2016/679 of the European Parliament and of the Council of 27 April 2016 on the protection of natural persons with regard to the processing of personal data and on the free movement of such data, and repealing Directive 95/46/EC (General Data Protection Regulation), OJ 2016 L 119, p. 1.

33   Directive 95/46/EC of the European Parliament and of the Council of 24 October 1995 on the protection of individuals with regard to the processing of personal data and on the free movement of such data, OJ 1995 L 281, p. 31.

34   Cf. in this regard *Epiney/Kern,* Zu den Neuerungen im Datenschutzrecht der Europäischen Union, in: Epiney/Nüesch (eds.), Die Revision des Datenschutzes in Europa und die Schweiz/La révision de la protection des données en Europe et la Suisse, 2016, p. 39 f. (72 f.).

35   UNTS

36   See for further details, *Epiney/Metz/Pirker* (note 2), p. 191 f.

constitutes an important (but not sufficient) argument in favour of such a parallel interpretation.

– Second, the context of the Bilateral Agreements calls for such a parallel interpretation since the agreements form a sort of network providing for a real but in some sort limited "integration" of Switzerland into the EU acquis.

– Third, – and this may be the decisive argument – most of the Bilateral Agreements (and generally those which take over EU law) involve a partial integration of Switzerland into the relevant EU *acquis* as a fundamental objective. This integration, however, can only be realised in an effective manner if the relevant parts of the agreements are interpreted in the same way as in EU law, thus integrating the rulings of the ECJ. Some agreements (e.g. Art. 16 (2) of the Agreement on Free Movement of Persons) therefore explicitly provide for an obligation for Switzerland to interpret articles of the agreement referring to EU law in the same way as the ECJ does in its rulings. Even if this obligation is limited to rulings given prior to the signature of the agreement, this does not mean that later rulings are irrelevant since the very objective of the agreement (parallel legal situation) suggests they are to be regarded as being of certain relevance.

As a result, one may formulate the principle that Bilateral Agreements must be interpreted parallel to the relevant articles/secondary legislation in EU law if the latter has been integrated into the agreement and if the aim of the relevant parts of the agreement is precisely to guarantee a parallel legal situation. In other words, if the objective is to extend the relevant EU law *acquis* to Switzerland to provide for a participation of Switzerland in the defined/relevant part of the EU *acquis*, the Bilateral Agreement is to be interpreted in the same way as the relevant EU law. This principle of parallel interpretation is – considering the overall objective of parallelism – not limited to a static situation at the time of signature but must be understood in a dynamic way, seeing, as only such an approach is able to achieve the aim of parallelism.

However, there are some difficulties in the concrete application of the principle. Three main points may be mentioned in this context:

– First, the principle only sets a general framework; it does not provide a detailed analysis of the concrete legal question. Hence, a case-by-case examination is necessary and, in this context, the question if and to what extent a concrete article contained in the Bilateral Agreements truly incorporates EU law will very often be crucial and the answer to this question is not always clear in advance.

- Second, with respect to the rulings of the ECJ, the decisions must be analysed to determine which parts are relevant for the interpretation of the Bilateral Agreements. For example, following the rulings based on the concept of European citizenship is not possible since this concept was not taken up in the Agreement on Free Movement of Persons. However, since some rights conferred on European citizens are taken up in the Agreement in the same way, those aspects of the rulings are, in principle, also to be considered when interpreting the relevant articles of the Agreement.

- Finally, one must remember the lack of parallelism in some fields covered by the Bilateral Agreements since amendments of EU law have not been integrated into said agreements. This situation may raise the question of which parts of the "*old*" EU law have retained their validity also in the light of the amended EU legislation so that, for example, the relevant rulings of the ECJ can also still be of some importance in the framework of the agreements.

Despite all these questions and difficulties, one must admit that, overall, the agreements work rather well. It seems that the ECJ and the Federal Supreme Court in Switzerland (*Bundesgericht*) apply the principles developed before, even if at time the focus may be different. The practice of the two courts – which almost exclusively concerns the Agreement on Free Movement of Persons – has also seen some developments and has become clearer over time.

The ECJ has certainly pointed out the specificities of the EU–Swiss relationship, in particular the Swiss decision not to participate in the EEA and to pursue another way and a lower degree of integration, in its first rulings on the Agreement on the Free Movement of Persons without, however, really dealing with the above-mentioned questions.[37] However, the latest case law has taken a different approach. It finally argues in favour of a principle of parallel interpretation, also raising the question of whether concepts or notions of EU law are really integrated into the agreement. In this sense, the Court argued that Switzerland is linked to the EU by a multitude of agreements covering various areas and containing rights and obligations corresponding to those contained in EU law. Hence, the overall objective of those agreements is to intensify the economic relations between the contracting parties. On this basis, and by referring also to its own rulings after the signature of the agreement, the Court has argued – in relation to the relevant articles in the agreement – in the same way as it does in the framework of EU

---

37   Cf. in particular ECJ, *Grimme*, Case C-351/08, EU:C:2009:697; ECJ, *Fokus Invest*, Case C-541/08, EU:C:2010:74; ECJ, *Hengartner*, Case C-70/09, EU:C:2010:430.

law, for example concerning the inclusion of indirect discrimination in the concept of discrimination, the interpretation of "public order" as a derogation from the guaranteed freedoms, the relevance of the principle of free movement in relation to tax law or provisions in the field of social security.[38] In one case, the ECJ even pointed out that the preamble and Art. 16 para. 2 of the Agreement on the Free Movement of Persons lead to the conclusion that a parallel legal situation between the EU, on the one side, and Switzerland, on the other, is intended by the agreement and that thus, in principle, the rulings of the ECJ are relevant. It applies this approach to Art. 2 of the Agreement (the principle of non-discrimination), which is interpreted parallel to Art. 18 TFEU.[39]

The Federal Supreme Court of Switzerland has already been called to interpret and apply the Agreement on the Free Movement of Persons on many occasions. It developed the principle that central concepts, notions and provisions of the agreement were carried over from EU law and ought to be interpreted and applied in conformity with the case law of the ECJ, which in theory includes the case law developed after the signature of the agreement.[40] The Supreme Court has even explicitly formulated this concept, mainly referring to the aims of the agreement, and has recently confirmed this approach despite some new provisions in the Federal Constitution potentially being in conflict with the Agreement on the Free Movement of Persons.[41] Therefore, one can conclude that the case law of the Federal Supreme Court applies the principle of parallel interpretation in a very consistent manner, an approach that is generally approved by the doctrine.[42]

---

38   Cf. ECJ, *Graf*, Case C-506/10, EU:C:2011:643; ECJ, *Bergström*, Case C-257/10, EU:C:2011:839; ECJ, *Ettwein*, Case C-425/11, EU:C:2013:121; ECJ, *Wagener*, Case C-250/13, EU:C:2014:278. See also the general remarks on the interpretation of the Agreement on Free Movement of Persons in ECJ, *UK/Council*, Case C-656/11, EU:C:2014:97.

39   ECJ, *Bukovansky*, Case C-241/14, EU:C:2015:766; in the same direction ECJ, *Radgen*, Case C-478/15, EU:C:2016:705.

40   See Federal Supreme Court, Case 2C_196/2009, *X. und Y. gegen Sicherheitsdirektion und Regierungsrat des Kantons Zürich*, BGE 136 II 5.

41   Federal Supreme Court, Case 2C_716/2014, *A.A. und B.A. gegen Migrationsamt und Sicherheitsdirektion des Kantons Zürich*, BGE 142 II 35.

42   See e. g. *Pirker*, Zu den für die Auslegung der Bilateralen Abkommen massgeblichen Grundsätzen – Gedanken zu BGE 140 II 112 (Gerichtsdolmetscher), Schweizerisches Zentralblatt für Staats- und Verwaltungsrecht, 2015, p. 295 (296 f.); *Maiani*, La „saga Metock", ou des inconvénients du pragmatisme helvétique dans la gestion des rapports entre droit européen, droit bilatéral et droit interne, Zeitschrift für Sozialreform, 2011, vol. I, p. 27 f.; *Oesch*, Der Einfluss des EU-

However, these principles – even if guaranteeing in general a good functioning of the Agreements – do not change the fact that access to justice and dispute settlement follow the "traditional" principles of Public International Law. Therefore, each party is responsible for access to justice (without a mechanism like the preliminary ruling) and there is no dispute settlement between the parties. This situation implies a risk of different interpretation and application of the Agreements.

D. Institutional Questions

For several years know, there have been discussions regarding the institutional framework of the Bilateral Agreements. Official negotiations in the matter started in 2014 and are still ongoing.[43] The issue at core is the EU's demand that homogeneity is ensured as far as market access agreements are concerned or, in other words, the EU's stance that Switzerland must adhere to the rules of the internal market when and where it wishes to take part in it. In this context, the EU demands consistency not only of the content of the law but also of its development, interpretation and thus application. Thereof essentially four main institutional matters or questions are derived: First, the

---

Rechts auf die Schweiz – von Gerichtsdolmetschern, Gerichtsgutachten und Notaren, Schweizerische Juristen-Zeitung, 2016, p. 53 f.; in detail also *Epiney/Metz/Pirker* (note 2), p. 169 f. See for a summary and analysis of the relevant rulings of the *Bundesgericht* the regular reports in the *Jahrbuch für Migrationsrecht*, recently *Epiney/Nüesch*, Zur schweizerischen Rechtsprechung zum Personenfreizügigkeitsabkommen, in: Achermann et al. (eds.), Jahrbuch für Migrationsrecht/Annuaire du droit de la migration 2017/2018, 2018, p. 273 f.

43   In the light of the most recent developments in Swiss domestic politics the further continuation of the negotiations has become slightly unclear. The basic problem is that the EU has made a point of stating that certain of the so-called "flanking measures" which Switzerland introduced in order to secure wage protection (and which are supposed to "flank" the effects of the Agreement on the Free Movement of Persons) are no longer to be upheld in their current form and connected this with the negotiations regarding the institutional questions. In the wake of national discussions, the federation of the Swiss trade unions declared their refusal to take part in discussions, thus prompting some observers to state that the negotiations have factually come to an end. See e.g. NZZ of 9 August 2018, Die unheilige Allianz der Abschotter droht das Rahmenabkommen zu Fall zu bringen: „Mit dem Gesprächsboykott sind die Verhandlungen zwischen Bern und Brüssel über ein Rahmenabkommen wohl vorderhand gescheitert". However, there is no official statement of any sort in the matter and negotiations are thus officially still ongoing.

issue illustrated above regarding the updating of the agreement, thus the question of the mechanism put in place to adjust the agreements to developments of the EU *acquis* that has been integrated into the agreements; second, the question of how to ensure consistent interpretation of the agreements which has also been discussed above; third, the question of how supervision monitoring compliance with the Bilateral Agreements is ensured and, lastly, the question of what procedures should be used to settle disputes between the parties to the agreements.[44] The aim of a framework agreement would thus be to set down the answers to these questions in an overarching manner or, in other words, finally for future and possibly current (market access) agreements. In the following, several specific issues shall be addressed in this regard. In this context, references to the negotiations between Switzerland and the EU will be made. It is, however, important to point out that these negotiations are ongoing which means that, firstly, information regarding the content of a possible agreement is rather sparse in certain areas and that, secondly, even if information has been distributed, essentially by the Swiss Federal Council who in some instances has stated that consensus has been reached on certain issues, account must be taken of the fact that "nothing is agreed until everything is agreed".

First, the scope of application of an institutional framework agreement is to be determined. It namely needs to be defined whether the new agreement would be applicable also to existing agreements, thus possibly contradicting or implementing changes to the agreements' proper approaches to the institutional issues, or if the scope of application would be restricted to new, future market access agreements. Currently, it appears that according to the ongoing negotiations the agreement would not only be applicable to agreements concluded in the future, but also to certain existing market access agreements, namely the Agreements on the Free Movement of Persons, on Land Transport, on Air Transport, on Trade in Agricultural Products and on

---

44   On the legal questions surrounding an institutional framework agreement in general, further *Oesch/Speck,* Das geplante institutionelle Abkommen Schweiz–EU und der EuGH, in: Epiney/Hehemann (eds.), Schweizerisches Jahrbuch für Europarecht 2016/2017, 2017, p. 257 f.; *Oesch* (note 2), p. 165 f.; *de Sépibus,* Ein institutionelles Dach für die Beziehungen zwischen der Schweiz und der Europäischen Union: Wie weiter?, in: Epiney/Diezig, Schweizerisches Jahrbuch für Europarecht 2013/2014, 2014, p. 397 f.; in detail also *Mazille,* L'institutionnalisation de la relation entre l'Union européenne et la Suisse: Recherche sur une construction européenne, 2018, p. 456 f.

the Mutual Recognition of Conformity Assessments.[45] Thus, not all existing market access agreements would fall into the scope of application of a future institutional framework agreement and it was seemingly possible to negotiate a limitation in this regard.

Second, addressing the question of decision shaping is necessary. According to the Swiss Federal Council, consensus has been found as to the procedure of updating the agreements. Any "automatism" in the sense that certain developments in EU law would automatically be binding also for Switzerland has seemingly been ruled out. Rather, one should put in place a dynamic system. Thus, agreements would need to be adjusted to developments taking place at EU level, but Switzerland could follow its own legislative process in this context, thus like the existing system in the Schengen Association Agreement. If, however, Switzerland failed to take over the relevant EU legal acts, the relevant agreement would not, unlike in the case of the Schengen Association Agreement, automatically be deemed suspended, but the other party could rather take compensatory measures. In the sense of an "institutional counterbalance"[46], such a procedure, however, entails with it the demand that certain decision-shaping rights are put in place. It appears probable that the future mechanism would be inspired by existing systems, such as, e.g., in the Schengen Association Agreement. However, to date and as far as can be seen, there have not been any statements as to what can be expected from an institutional framework agreement in this regard. In any case, rights will be restricted to simple participation in EU legislative procedures and any decision-making rights are not to be expected. Nevertheless, the impact that possibilities of decision shaping by Switzerland can have, are not to be underestimated. For instance, regarding the amendments to Directive 91/477/EEC on control of acquisition and possession of weapons,[47] which has been judged relevant for the Schengen *acquis* and the Schengen Association Agreement

---

45   Press conference of the Federal Council of 5 March 2018, where it was confirmed that consensus has been reached as regards the restriction of the framework agreements scope of application to these five specific agreements and future market access agreements.

46   *Federal Council,* Bericht in Erfüllung des Postulats Hans Fehr 10.3857 of 1.10.2010: Konsequenzen des Schengen-Anpassungszwangs, 7.6.2013, BBl 2013, p. 6319 f. (6332); see also *Oesch,* Die bilateralen Abkommen Schweiz – EU und die Übernahme von EU-Recht, AJP 2017 638 (643).

47   Council Directive 91/477/EEC of 18 June 1991 on control of the acquisition and possession of weapons, OJ 1991 L 256, p. 51 as amended by Directive (EU) 2017/853 of the European Parliament and the Council of 17 May 2017 amending Council Directive 91/477/EEC on control of the acquisition and possession of weapons, OJ 2017 L 137, p. 22.

could thus be suspended if Switzerland refuses to take over the new legislation, Switzerland succeeded in giving the respective amendments a "Swiss finish". It namely appeared possible for Switzerland to persuade the EU legislator to introduce an exception regarding members of the military who, as is customary in Switzerland, can keep their weapons at home, even after having fulfilled their military duty. Art. 6 para. 6 Directive 91/477/EEC now foresees that "Member States applying a military system based on general conscription and having in place over the last 50 years a system of transfer of military firearms to persons leaving the army after fulfilling their military duties may grant to those persons, in their capacity as a target shooter, an authorisation to keep one firearm used during the mandatory military period." This illustrates nicely how Switzerland was able to apply its rights of decision shaping to introduce a "Swiss" provision into an EU legal act.[48]

Furthermore, a question discussed rather intensely, at least in public discussion, is the one regarding dispute settlement. This currently also remains an open question, which is still being negotiated. However, it seems that progress in this regard has been made. According to the Federal Council, Switzerland suggested the implementation of an arbitration system, after this was first introduced to the discussion by the EU Commission's president in the framework of an official visit to Switzerland.[49] Thus, according to the Federal Council's proposition, disputes would be brought before an arbitral tribunal. In a first step, this tribunal would then assess the question of whether the disposition(s) relevant to the dispute constituted EU law or "proper" bilateral law. This can already pose problems. The arbitral tribunal would thus need to determine whether a disposition in question is to be seen as a provision copying EU law, thus a "copy-paste-provision" or whether the disposition in question is an "autonomous article" created in or by the negotiations between the treaty parties. It appears easily imaginable that this could be more difficult in practice as it may seem to be on paper. If the arbitral tribunal deems the disposition as constituting EU law, the Court of Justice of the European Union would be asked to decide on the interpretation of the disposition in question and the arbitral tribunal would issue its decision only afterwards, bound by the interpretation laid down by the ECJ. Apart from raising

---

48   See in this regard also *Oesch* (note. 45), p. 645 f.
49   Press release of the Federal Council 5 March 2018, https://www.eda.admin.ch/dea/de/home/aktuell/medienmitteilungen.html/content/dea/de/meta/news/2018/3/5/69970 (last accessed on 26 September 2018); NZZ of 28 December 2017, EU bringt eine Schiedsgericht-Lösung ins Spiel.

the difficulty of having to distinguish dispositions of "copied" EU law and other dispositions in the agreement, this proposal also raises the question of whether such a procedure would be regarded as compatible with EU law in light of the principle of autonomy of EU law developed by the ECJ.[50] In relation to the question of different entities deciding on disputes possibly based on EU law, the principle of autonomy of EU law seemingly means that the ECJ must be responsible for the interpretation of any EU law disposition. The court seems to have confirmed this position in a recent ruling with relation to the question of the competences of an arbitral tribunal in investor-to-state disputes, as foreseen by an agreement between two Member States. The court seems to state that, if a tribunal is to resolve disputes which are "liable to relate to the interpretation or application of EU law"[51], this tribunal must constitute either a court or tribunal of a Member State within the meaning of Art. 267 TFEU – which would mean it could submit questions to the ECJ – or its decisions must be subject to review by a court of a Member State, which would again mean that questions of EU law could be submitted to ECJU.[52] To what extent the conclusions from said ruling regarding investor-to-state dispute settlement can be transferred to state-to-state dispute settlement and to agreements concluded between the EU and third states, and thus to the issue of the dispute settlement between Switzerland and the EU, is unclear.[53] In any case, it appears safe to conclude that any procedure put in place in an institutional framework agreement must ensure that the final interpretation of EU law is decided upon by the ECJ. It also appears imaginable that the ECJs jurisprudence relating to the principle of autonomy of EU law could

---

50   Cf. in this regard ECJ, *EEA I*, Opinion 1/91,EU:C:1991:490, para 30 f.; ECJ, *EEA II*, Opinion 1/92, EU:C:1992:189, para 18 f.; ECJ, *European Patents Court*, Opinion 1/09, EU:C:2011:123, in particular para 67 f.; ECJ, *Accession to the ECHR*, Opinion 2/13, EU:C:2014:2454, in particular para 179 f.; cf. regarding the latter also *Pirker/Reitemeyer,* Between Discursive and Exclusive Autonomy – Opinion 2/13, the Protection of Fundamental Rights and the Autonomy of EU Law, Cambridge Yearbook of European Legal Studies 2015, 168 f.

51   ECJ, *Achmea*, Case C-284/16, EU:C:2018:158, para 39.

52   ECJ, *Achmea*, Case C-284/16, EU:C:2018:158, para 39 f.; cf. in this regard also *Ankersmit,* Dispute settlement in the current generation of trade and investment agreements of the EU: departing from the days of caution and restraint?, in: Epiney/Hehemann, Schweizerisches Jahrbuch für Europarecht 2017/2018, 2018, p. 365 (375 f.).

53   Cf. *Glaser/Döring*, Die Streitbeilegung in den Bilateralen Abkommen Schweiz–EU, in: Epiney/Hehemann, (note 51), p. 451 f. (462); *Muser/Tobler*, Schiedsgerichte in den Aussenverträgen der EU: Neue Entwicklungen unter Einbezug der institutionellen Verhandlungen Schweiz–EU, Jusletter of 28 May 2018.

mean that it would need to be possible for one treaty party to request a ruling of the ECJ on the question whether the relevant provision of the Bilateral Agreements contains EU law. In this case, if the arbitral tribunal should decide that the provision relevant to the dispute constituted genuine bilateral law and not EU law, the treaty parties would have the possibility to challenge this decision before the ECJ. To date, it seems no information on whether the EU plans to introduce such an option in an institutional framework agreement has been communicated.[54] A look at the ECJs jurisprudence on the autonomy of EU law – and especially the latest ruling that even disputes *liable* to relate to EU law must be brought before the ECJ – reveals, however, that it cannot be deemed unlikely that granting an arbitral tribunal the final say on whether a provision constitutes EU law or not could be regarded as contrary to EU law.

Furthermore, the question raises as to what the consequences are when detecting a lack of homogeneity. One probable answer seems to be that one treaty party could take compensatory measures towards the other party, at least according to the information issued by the Swiss Federal Council. These would then need to be in line with the principle of proportionality, a general principle of law, which, in turn, constitutes a source of international law in the sense of Art. 38 para. 1 Statute of the International Court of Justice.[55] Whether this principle is respected in the concrete case could again be assessed by the arbitral tribunal as proposed in the context of a possible mechanism for dispute settlement. For this assessment of the proportionality of the compensatory measures, certain guidelines could possibly be laid down in an institutional framework agreement. As an *ultima ratio* with regard to a lack of homogeneity, the institutional framework agreement could possibly foresee that a treaty party could terminate the agreement in question. With regard

---

54   See also *Muser/Tobler* (note 52) who point out that the EU Commission has included this option in the system proposed in its draft of a withdrawal agreement between the UK and the EU presented in February 2018. Art. 162 of this draft foresees that a dispute concerning the interpretation or application of the agreement is to be brought before a joint committee. This joint committee may, however, decide to submit the dispute to the ECJ for a binding ruling or, if the joint committee does not do so and fails to settle the dispute within three months, either the EU or the UK are entitled to submit the dispute to the ECJ. The text of the Commission's draft withdrawal agreement is available at <https://ec.europa.eu/commission/publications/draft-withdrawal-agreement-withdrawal-united-kingdom-great-britain-and-northern-ireland-european-union-and-european-atomic-energy-community_en> (last accessed on 26 September 2018).

55   Cf. *Crawford*, Proportionality, in: Wolfrum, The Max Planck Encyclopedia of Public International Law, 2012, para 1.

to the already existing agreements that would possibly be covered by a framework agreement, this would, at least according to the current structure, mean that all five would be terminated, since they are all connected by the so-called "guillotine clause", stating that the termination of one of the agreements concluded in the context of the Bilateral Agreements I leads to the termination of the other agreements of this package.[56]

Finally, from a political point of view, it appears justified to ask where the main differences opposed to EU membership or being member of the EEA – which Switzerland rejected in a popular vote in 1992 – lie if all of the EU's demands were met, thus if Switzerland were to (more or less) completely adhere to the rules of the internal market in the relevant areas by, in particular, taking over developments of EU law (or else risking being the target of compensatory measures) and accepting the authority of the ECJ to interpret EU law contained in the agreements. It essentially raises the question whether the relationship between the EU and Switzerland really is void of supranational elements – as this appears to be one main reason behind Switzerland's choice of the "bilateral path" – or whether, at least in certain areas, Switzerland factually plays the role of a Member State without any decision-making powers. In the end it results in a political decision whether a state chooses to go "all in" and thus be able to take part in the making of decisions or whether it rather prefers to "stay outside" and to pay the price of having to adhere to rules without having any voting rights in the matter if it still wants to profit from the internal market.

E.   *Possible or Probable Characteristics of the "Swiss Model"*

With regard to the relationship between the UK and the EU after Brexit, an examination whether the Bilateral Agreements between Switzerland and the EU could possibly serve as a model would be useful.[57] In this context, the

---

56   See, e. g., Art. 25 para. 4 of the Agreement on the Free Movement of Persons.
57   Cf. in this context also *Tobler,* One of Many Challenges After 'BREXIT': The Institutional Framework of an Alternative Agreement – Lessons from Switzerland and Elsewhere?, Maastricht Journal of European and Comparative Law 2016, p. 575 f.; *Breitenmoser/Jutzeler,* Das bilaterale Verhältnis der EU mit der Schweiz als pragmatische Lösung für den Brexit?, in: Hilpold (ed.), Europa im Umbruch, Europarecht Beiheft 1, 2017, p. 77 f.; *Reber,* Swiss Bilateral Agreements with the EU as an inspiration for a future UK–EU relationship?, in: Kellerhals/Baumgartner (eds.), New dynamics in the European integration process – Europe post Brexit, 2018, p. 143 f.; *Epiney,* Die Beziehungen Schweiz – EU als Modell für die

main characteristics of the Bilateral Agreements as they were set out above and the demands of the EU with regard to the institutional questions shall be presented before the background of the situation of the UK, thus laying down the framework which would probably need to be respected if the UK should wish to follow the "Swiss path".

– First, a crucial question when discussing the possible future relationship between the EU and the UK is the one regarding the exact amplitude of one or more possible agreement(s). The EU's demand regarding market access appears rather clear: Either one adheres to the internal market with all its facets or one remains outside of the internal market. In this sense, the EU has made a point of repeatedly stating that so-called cherry picking is not an option.[58] In this regard, it is important to note that the very sectoral approach of the Bilateral Agreements between Switzerland and the EU was taken before the historical background of trying to work towards an accession of Switzerland to the EU. It is thus imaginable that the EU would not be willing to take the same path again, especially not regarding a state withdrawing and not likely to accede to the Union soon.

– Furthermore, the Bilateral Agreements – or at least the agreements aiming at gaining market access – are mainly linked to the requirement of taking over EU law or, in other words, the EU *acquis* and its developments in the relevant sector. However, as the example of the Schengen and Dublin Association Agreements shows and as it has also become clear in the negotiations regarding an institutional framework agreement, this does not preclude Switzerland of following its ordinary legislative process. A certain timeframe is granted for this. Whilst the Schengen and Dublin Association Agreements foresee a period of two years, Switzerland apparently succeeded in negotiating a period of three years in the context of a possible institutional framework agreement, in the light of the fact that legislation

---

Gestaltung des Verhältnisses Großbritanniens zur EU?, in: Kramme/Baldus/Schmidt-Kessel (eds.), Brexit und die juristischen Folgen, 2017, p. 77 f. on which the following section is partially based.

58   See for instance European Council (Art. 50) guidelines on the framework for the future EU–UK relationship of 23 March 2018, EUCO XT 20001/18, nr. 7: "The European Council recalls that the four freedoms are indivisible and that there can be no 'cherry-picking' through participation in the Single Market based on a sector-by-sector approach, which would undermine the integrity and proper functioning of the Single Market."

is a slow-moving process, partly due to the system of direct democracy.[59]

– Regarding the updating of (a) possible agreement(s) in line with developments of the relevant EU *acquis*, the question also arises whether certain exceptions could be foreseen. As it is shown about the scope of the Bilateral Agreements between Switzerland and the EU, Switzerland is not bound to take over all developments and was able to negotiate certain exceptions. For instance, one can state that Switzerland participates, at least to a certain extent, in the system of the free movement of persons but has not taken over Directive 2004/38/EC, the so-called citizenship directive. This is, however, due to the static nature of the Agreement on the Free Movement of Persons, which requires consensus about the updating of the agreement to developments at EU law level. When looking at the EU's demands in relation to an institutional framework agreement, which appear to rather clearly state that Switzerland is to take over EU law developments in the realm of market access agreements, it does not appear very probable that the current "Swiss model" of having such static agreements could be copied as it stands.

– Regarding the situation between Switzerland and the EU, it has also been shown that it is currently still unclear what the consequences are when developments of EU law are not adopted despite being bound to do so. According to the negotiations regarding a framework agreement, this would mean that compensatory measures – which would need to respect the principle of proportionality – could be taken.

– With the EU's requirement of laying down an obligation to take over EU law and its developments, come, on the other side of the coin, certain decision-shaping rights. In this regard it appears that the EU seems willing to grant the respective third states certain rights of participation in meetings of the council or commission committees.

– Apart from the requirement of taking over the relevant EU *acquis* including its developments, the principle of parallel interpretation and application as it was illustrated above is also to be pointed out in this context. This appears to be a central aspect of agreements between the EU and third states, at least where a certain amount of integration of the respective state into the EU internal market is in-

---

59   See NZZ, Die EU kommt der Schweiz entgegen, 9 April 2018.

tended. Thus, it would need to be ensured that provisions of (a) possible agreement(s) which incorporate EU law with the objective of creating a parallel legal situation are interpreted (and thus applied) in the same way as the respective EU law is in the Union. This entails a certain obligation to take account of already existing case law of the ECJ at the point of signature of an agreement as well as its developments.

- This, in turn, raises the issue of the surveillance over the correct interpretation and application of the agreement(s) – which includes the principle – and the settlement of possible disputes. In this regard, it appears that the preferred option of the EU would be to designate the ECJ with a strong role in the matter. However, it also seems possible to foresee an option with an arbitral tribunal, nevertheless leaving the interpretation of EU law in the hands of the ECJ. The latter does not seem negotiable in the light of the principle of the autonomy of EU law as developed by the ECJ.

- Finally, it is to be pointed out that a lack of homogeneity possibly could lead to a termination of the agreement(s). In other words, in the areas of the internal market concerned by the agreement(s), the UK would need to adhere to EU law regarding the matter in question, at least to a significant extent, if the functioning of the agreement(s) should be ensured.

F.   *Excursus: Relationship UK – Third Countries*

Regarding Brexit, questions arise regarding the future relationship not only with the EU but also with third states such as Switzerland, a relationship that, as shown, is currently mostly regulated by treaties concluded between the EU (and its Member States) and Switzerland. If the treaty in question is a non-mixed treaty, it becomes clear that the UK – no longer forming part of the EU – will cease to be a treaty party when Brexit comes into force. In the case of mixed treaties, such as, for example, the Agreement on the Free Movement of Persons between the EU and its Member States on the one hand and Switzerland on the other hand, the case does not appear quite as clear at a first glance since the UK itself is also a treaty party and not only the Union.[60] Thus, the conclusion could be drawn that a withdrawal from the EU would

---

60   The following is partially based on *Epiney,* "Brexit" und FZA: Zu den Perspektiven der Freizügigkeit zwischen der Schweiz und der EU im Gefolge des "Brexit", Jusletter of 20.3.2017.

not change anything with regard to the status of the UK as a treaty partner. As concerns the Agreement on the Free Movement of Persons, such a conclusion is, however, to be rejected. The UK is a treaty partner solely due to its role as Member State, as this already becomes clear from the title of the agreement. The agreement does not foresee that there could be any other treaty partners other than the EU and its Member States on the one side and Switzerland on the other side and can thus be described as a "closed" agreement. Such an interpretation is also in line with the general aim of the agreement, which, according to the preamble of the agreement, is to "bring about the free movement of persons between [the treaty partners] based on the rules applying in the European Community". If a Member State withdraws from the Union, the EU law rules, which form the basis of the agreement, cease to apply to this state and it can thus no longer be viewed as part of the "EU pillar". Thus, at least as far as the Agreement on the Free Movement of Persons with Switzerland is concerned, it can be stated that the UK will no longer be a treaty partner after Brexit.[61]

In this regard, questions arise as to the future of individual rights acquired due to the agreement or in the process of being acquired. Generally, international agreements no longer have any legal effects once they cease to be in force. Treaty parties might foresee exemptions to this rule in the agreement in question, as this was made for the Agreement on the Free Movement of Persons. Art. 23 of said agreement foresees that rights acquired by private individuals shall not be affected in the case of a termination or non-renewal of the agreement.[62] With regard to rights in the process of being acquired, the treaty parties are to mutually agree on what action is to be taken. It can be argued that the provision also applies regarding British citizens having acquired rights based on the agreement in Switzerland and vice versa. While the provision was arguably intended to regulate the situation of the whole

---

61   Cf. for the same conclusion regarding the EEA Agreement, with a slightly different reasoning, *Sif Tynes/Haugsdal*, In: Out or In-between? The UK as a Contracting Party to the Agreement on the European Economic Area, 41 (2016) European Law Review, 753 f. (763).

62   Cf. in this regard *Borghi*, La libre circulation des personnes entre la Suisse et l'UE: Commentaire article par article de l'accord du 21 juin 1999, Art. 23, *passim*; *Blaser*, Commentary of Art. 23, in: Amarelle/Nguyen (eds.), Code annoté de droit des migrations: Volume III: Accord sur la libre circulation des personnes (ALCP), *passim*; also *Tobler*, After 'BREXIT': will rights acquired in the context of the free movement of persons be protected? A comparative perspective, Revista de Direito Constitucional e Internacional 2017, p. 349 f.; *Tobler*, Und wenn das Abkommen wegfällt? Erworbene Rechte nach Art. 23 FZA, in: Achermann et al. (eds.), Jahrbuch für Migrationsrecht 2015/2016, 2016, p. 43 f.

treaty being terminated, it can also be applied in this case, since the aim of the provision is to protect individuals' rights already acquired or which are in the process of being acquired. In addition, this concern matters not only when the whole treaty is terminated but also when it ceases to apply only about the relationship between Switzerland and one former EU Member State.

It appears clear that there is a certain need to think about the design of the relationship between the UK and third countries, such as Switzerland, after treaties concluded between the EU and these third states, e.g. the Bilateral Agreements between the EU and Switzerland, will have ceased to apply in the relationship with the UK. In this context, several scenarios appear possible. On the one hand, there could be no agreements regulating the relationship. Regarding the issue of the free movement of persons, this does not appear very probable as this would mean a significant step back about the rights of individuals and currently does not appear to be in the interest of any party. On the other hand, and this appears more likely, the UK and Switzerland could conclude a new agreement. As regards the content, it could take over the principles of the existing agreement between Switzerland and the EU and the latter either's Member States or contain "new", autonomously agreed upon provisions. Taking over the principles of the current agreement would entail the advantage that the existing situation could continue and that a certain degree of legal certainty could be upheld, seeing that many question regarding application and interpretation of the Agreement on the Free Movement of Persons have already been dealt with. However, this would also imply that the UK would, to a certain extent, still be bound by "EU law" since, as it has been shown, the Agreement on the Free Movement of Persons is largely based on principles and concepts of EU law. It remains to be seen whether the UK is willing to agree to such a solution from a political point of view as the question of the free movement of persons appears to be one of the main issues that led to the decision to withdraw from the EU (however, seemingly not regarding migration from Switzerland). Finally, the question also arises whether such an agreement between the UK and Switzerland would necessarily be concluded bilaterally or whether the conclusion of a trilateral agreement between the UK, Switzerland and the EU would be a possibility. This, however, would again entail that the UK were willing to subject itself to EU law to a certain extent.

G. Conclusion

In the following, the disadvantages and advantages the UK would be faced with when following the "Swiss model" are to be set out. The main disadvantage would probably be that a conclusion of agreements like the agreements concluded between the EU and Switzerland could, depending on the point of view, lead to a reduction of "sovereignty". This appears so in the light of the fact that the UK would probably be bound – legally or factually – to take over certain parts and the respective developments of EU law without having decision-making powers in this regard, to then apply these rules parallel to the way they are interpreted in the EU and to possibly, to a certain extent, be bound to follow the ECJ's rulings with regard to the relevant EU law. However, in this context it is important to point out that the decision to conclude such agreements with the EU, which would then lead to the mentioned situation, is to be a sovereign act, thus explaining why quotation marks are used in this context.

A further disadvantage could be seen in the overwhelming complexity of the "Swiss model". It has been shown that currently the relationship between Switzerland and the EU is guided by more than hundred bilateral agreements, some of which even constitute mixed agreements. Currently, these agreements all follow their own institutional structure, many with their own joint committees. This calls not only for a great deal of work on both sides, but also creates a situation where it becomes increasingly difficult to stay on top of things.

On the other side, the main advantage of a solution based on the "Swiss model" would be its "individuality". The agreement(s) would be concluded between the UK and the EU (and in certain areas possibly the latter's Member States) alone, thus allowing for the creation of specific solutions beneficial to the treaty parties. This appears as the main advantage in comparison to a solution based on an accession of the UK to the EEA, where the UK would be only one of four on one side of the negotiating table. At the same time, the "Swiss model" shows that participation at the internal market apparently remains possible, also with a tailor-made solution.

In the end, whether the UK should or will follow the "Swiss model" remains a political question, which is to be answered both on the part of the UK, but also on the part of the EU. Especially the latter will have to decide whether it is willing to take the same path again or whether it wants to keep regarding the relationship with Switzerland as an historical particularity, which is not to be repeated in this form. This decision might also be dependent on how the current negotiations between Switzerland and the EU on an institutional framework agreement turn out.

Authors

Affolter, Sian	Université de Fribourg, Freiburg i.Ue..
Anthony, Gordon	Prof., Queen's University, Belfast.
Arnull, Anthony	Prof., University of Birmingham, Birmingham.
Dawson, Mark	Prof., PhD., Hertie School of Governance, Berlin.
Epiney, Astrid	Prof. Dr., Université de Fribourg, Freiburg i.Ue..
Kadelbach, Stefan	Prof. Dr., LL.M. (University of Virginia), Goethe-Universität Frankfurt am Main, Frankfurt am Main.
Ruffert, Matthiass	Prof., Dr., Humboldt-Universität zu Berlin, Berlin.
Schewe, Christoph	Prof. Dr., M.E.S. (Salamanca), FHVD Kiel-Altenholz, Reinfeld.